Denis Florence McCarthy

**The Book of Irish Ballads**

Denis Florence McCarthy

**The Book of Irish Ballads**

ISBN/EAN: 9783743327269

Manufactured in Europe, USA, Canada, Australia, Japa

Cover: Foto ©Thomas Meinert / pixelio.de

Manufactured and distributed by brebook publishing software (www.brebook.com)

Denis Florence McCarthy

**The Book of Irish Ballads**

TO

SAMUEL FERGUSON, Esq., M.R.I.A,

BARRISTER-AT-LAW,

HIS COLLECTION

OF

IRISH BALLADS,

ENRICHED BY SO MANY BEAUTIFUL EFFORTS OF
HIS GENIUS,

IS RESPECTFULLY INSCRIBED

BY

THE EDITOR.

# CONTENTS.

| | | |
|---|---|---|
| DEDICATION, | | 3 |
| INDEX OF AUTHORS, | | 5 |
| ADVERTISEMENT. | | 10 |
| INTRODUCTION, | | 11 |

## BALLADS ILLUSTRATIVE OF THE FAIRY MYTHOLOGY AND TRADITIONS OF IRELAND.

| Names of Ballads. | Authors' Names. | Page |
|---|---|---|
| A Fairy Tale, | Thomas Parnell, | 25 |
| The Fairy Well of Lagnanay, | Samuel Ferguson, | 31 |
| Hy-Brasail, | Gerald Griffin, | 34 |
| The Mountain Sprite, | Thomas Moore, | 35 |
| The City of Gold, | Anonymous, | 36 |
| Thubber-na-Shie; or, The Fairy Well, | James Tecling, | 37 |
| Fairy Revels, | Anonymous, | 40 |
| The Enchanted Island, | Anonymous, | 41 |
| The Fairy Rath of Loch Innin, | Alexander Henry, | 42 |
| The Phantom City, | Gerald Griffin, | 43 |
| The Magic Well, | W. M. Downs, | 49 |
| Arranmore, | Thomas Moore, | 56 |
| The Island of Atlantis, | Rev. G. Croly, | 57 |
| The Haunted Spring, | Samuel Lover, | 59 |
| Alice and Una, | D. F. M'Carthy, | 60 |

## BALLADS ILLUSTRATIVE OF THE SUPERSTITIONS AND CUSTOMS OF IRELAND.

| | | |
|---|---|---|
| The Fetch, | John Banim, | 75 |
| The Banshee, | Anonymous, | 76 |
| Cusheen Loo, | J. J. Callanan, | 78 |
| The Burial, | Rev. J. Wills, | 79 |
| The O'Neill, | Anonymous, | 80 |
| The Wake of the Absent, | Gerald Griffin, | 84 |
| Kathleen's Fetch, | Anonymous, | 85 |
| The Doom of the Mirror, | B. Simmons, | 87 |
| The Fairy Nurse, | Edward Walsh | 91 |
| Earl Desmond and the Banshee, | Anonymous, | 92 |
| The Bridal Wake, | Gerald Griffin, | 95 |
| The Caoine, | Crofton Croker, | 96 |

## CONTENTS.

### HISTORICAL BALLADS.

| Names of Songs. | A.D. | Authors' Names. | Page |
|---|---|---|---|
| The Saga of King Olaf and his Dog, | 1000 | Thomas D'Arcy M'Gee, | 97 |
| Lamentation of Mac Liag for Kincora, | 1015 | James Clarence Mangan. | 102 |
| The Death of King Magnus Barefoot, | 1102 | Thomas D'Arcy M'Gee, | 104 |
| Battle of Cnoctuadh, | 1189 | - - | 107 |
| A Vision of Connaught in the 13th Century, | 1224 | James Clarence Mangan, | 114 |
| Battle of Credran, | 1257 | Edward Walsh, | 116 |
| Battle of Ardnocker, | 1328 | * * * | 119 |
| Grainne Maol and Elizabeth, | 1575 | * * * | 122 |
| The Death of Schomberg, | 1690 | Digby Pilot Starkey, | 127 |
| The Battle of the Boyne, | 1690 | Colonel Blacker, | 129 |

### DESCRIPTIVE BALLADS.

| | | |
|---|---|---|
| Timoleague, | Samuel Ferguson. | 133 |
| Avondhu, | J. J. Callanan, | 136 |
| The Rock of Cashel, | Rev. Dr. Murray, | 137 |
| Loch Ina, | Anonymous, | 140 |
| The Returned Exile, | B. Simmons, | 141 |
| Glenfinishk, | Joseph O'Leary, | 143 |
| The Mountain Fern, | * * * | 145 |
| Adare, | Gerald Griffin. | 146 |
| The Vale of Shanganah, | D. F. M'Carthy, | 148 |
| Deirdre's Farewell to Alba, | Samuel Ferguson, | 150 |
| A Sigh for Knockmany, | William Carleton, | 151 |
| Tipperary, | Fionnuala, | 152 |

### LEGENDARY BALLADS.

| | | |
|---|---|---|
| The Welshmen of Tirawley, | Samuel Ferguson, | 154 |
| The Outlaw of Loch Lene, | J. J. Callanan, | 165 |
| Ailleen the Huntress, | Edward Walsh, | 166 |
| Shane Dyma's Daughter, | Anonymous, | 169 |
| O'Sullivan Beare, | Thomas D'Arcy M'Gee, | 173 |
| The Robber of Ferney, | Anonymous, | 176 |
| O'Donoghue's Bride, | Anonymous, | 178 |
| The Virgin Mary's Bank, | J. J. Callanan, | 179 |

## CONTENTS.

### BALLADS OF THE AFFECTIONS.

| Names of Songs. | Authors' Names. | Page |
|---|---|---|
| The Parting from Slemish, | Samuel Ferguson, | 181 |
| Ailleen, | J. Banim, | 183 |
| Eman-ac-Knuck to Eva, | J. B. Clarke, | 184 |
| O'Donnell and the Fair Fitzgerald, | Charles Gavan Duffy | 186 |
| The Coolun, | Samuel Ferguson, | 188 |
| Brighidin Ban Mo Stor, | Edward Walsh, | 190 |
| The Lamentation of Felix M'Carthy, | J. J. Callanan, | 191 |
| Pastheen Fion, | Samuel Ferguson, | 194 |
| The Patriot's Bride, | Charles Gavan Duffy, | 196 |
| The Coulin, | Caroll Malone, | 199 |
| Mauryeen, | Anonymous, | 201 |
| A Lament, | D. F. M'Carthy, | 202 |
| Young Kate of Kilcummer, | Anonymous, | 205 |
| The Mountain Dew, | Samuel Lover, | 206 |

### POLITICAL BALLADS.

| The Muster of the North, | Charles Gavan Duffy, | 207 |
|---|---|---|
| Dark Rosaleen, | James C. Mangan, | 211 |
| Drimin Dhu, | Samuel Ferguson, | 214 |
| Shane Bwee, | James C. Mangan, | ҄. |
| The Voice of Labour, | Charles Gavan Duffy. | 216 |
| The Dream of John M'Donnell, | James C Mangan, | 219 |
| The Wexford Insurgent, | Anonymous, | 222 |
| The Orangeman's Wife, | Caroll Malone, | 223 |
| The Irish Chiefs, | Charles Gavan Duffy | 225 |

### MISCELLANEOUS BALLADS.

| The Saint's Tenant, | Thomas Furlong, | 228 |
|---|---|---|
| Lament for the Sons of Usnach, | Samuel Ferguson, | 236 |
| The Penal Days, | Anonymous, | 239 |
| Carolan and Bridget Cruise, | Samuel Lover, | 243 |
| The Streams, | Mrs. Downing, | 245 |
| Irish Mary, | J. Banim, | 246 |
| The Last Friends, | Frances Browne, | 247 |
| The Irish Exiles, | Martin MacDermott. | 249 |

# INDEX OF AUTHORS.

### A

**ANONYMOUS:**

| | Page |
|---|---|
| The City of Gold | 36 |
| Fairy Revels | 40 |
| The Enchanted Island | 41 |
| The Banshee | 76 |
| The O'Neill | 80 |
| Kathleen's Fetch | 85 |
| Earl Desmond and the Banshee | 92 |
| Battle of Cnoctnadh | 107 |
| Battle of Ardnocker | 119 |
| Grainne Maol and Elizabeth | 122 |
| Loch Ina | 140 |
| The Mountain Fern | 145 |
| Tipperary | 152 |
| Shane Dymas' Daughter | 169 |
| The Robber of Ferney | 176 |
| O'Donoghue's Bride | 178 |
| Mauryeen | 201 |
| Kate of Kilcummer | 205 |
| The Wexford Insurgent | 222 |
| The Penal Days | 239 |

### B

**BANIM, JOHN:**

| | Page |
|---|---|
| The Fetch | 75 |
| Aileen | 183 |
| Irish Mary | 246 |

**BLACKER, COLONEL:**

| | Page |
|---|---|
| The Battle of the Boyne | 129 |

**BROWNE, FRANCES:**

| | Page |
|---|---|
| The Last Friends | 247 |

### C

**CALLANAN, J. J.**

| | Page |
|---|---|
| Cusheen Loo | 78 |
| Avondhu | 136 |
| The Outlaw of Loch Lene | 165 |
| The Virgin Mary's Bank | 179 |
| The Lamentation of Felix M'Carthy | 191 |

**CARLETON, WILLIAM:**

| | Page |
|---|---|
| A Sigh for Knockmany | 151 |

**CLARKE, J. B.:**

| | Page |
|---|---|
| Eman-ac-Knuck to Eva | 184 |

**CROKER, CROFTON:**

| | Page |
|---|---|
| The Caoine | 96 |

**CROLY, REV. GEORGE:**

| | Page |
|---|---|
| The Island of Atlantis | 57 |

### D

**DOWNES, W. M:**

| | Page |
|---|---|
| The Magic Well | 46 |

**DOWNING, MRS.:**

| | Page |
|---|---|
| The Streams | 245 |

**DUFFY, CHARLES GAVAN:**

| | Page |
|---|---|
| O'Donnell and the Fair Fitzgerald | 18 |
| The Patriot's Bride | 196 |
| The Muster of the North | 207 |
| The Voice of Labour | 214 |
| The Irish Chiefs | 221 |

# INDEX OF AUTHORS

## F

**FERGUSON, SAMUEL, M.R.I.A.**
- The Fairy Well of Lagnan — 31
- Timoleague — 133
- Deirdre's Farewell to Alba — 150
- The Welshmen of Tirawley — 154
- The Parting from Slemish — 181
- The Coolun — 188
- Pastheen Fion — 194
- Drimin Dhu — 214
- Lament for the Sons of Usnach — 236

**FURLONG, THOMAS:**
- The Saint's Tenant — 228

## G

**GRIFFIN, GERALD:**
- Hy-Brasail — 34
- The Phantom City — 48
- The Wake of the Absent — 84
- The Bridal Wake — 95
- Adare — 146

## H

**HENRY, ALEXANDER.**
- The Fairy Rath of Loch Innin — 42

## L

**LOVER, SAMUEL:**
- The Haunted Spring — 59
- The Mountain Dew — 206
- Carolan and Bridget Cruise — 243

## M

**M'CARTHY, D. F.:**
- Alice and Una — 60
- The Vale of Shanganah — 148
- A Lament — 202

**MACDERMOTT, MARTIN:**
- The Irish Exiles — 249

**M'GEE, THOMAS D'ARCY:**
- The Saga of King Olaf and his Dog — 97
- The Death of King Magnus Barefoot — 104
- O'Sullivan Beare — 173

## M

**MALONE, CARROLL:**
- The Coulin — 199
- The Orangeman's Wife — 228

**MANGAN, JAMES CLARENCE:**
- Lamentation of MacLiag for Kincora — 102
- A Vision of Connaught in the 13th Century — 114
- Dark Rosaleen — 211
- Shane Bwee — 214
- The Dream of John Mac Donnell — 219

**MOORE, THOMAS:**
- The Mountain Sprite — 35
- Arranmore — 56

**MURRAY, REV. DR.:**
- The Rock of Cashel — 137

## O

**O'LEARY, JOSEPH:**
- Glenfinishk — 143

## P

**PARNELL, THOMAS:**
- A Fairy Tale — 2

## S

**SIMMONS, B.**
- The Doom of the Mirror — 87
- The Returned Exile — 142

**STARKEY, DIGBY PILOT:**
- The Death of Schomberg — 127

## T

**TEELING, JAMES:**
- Thubber-na-Shie, or the Fairy Well — 37

## W

**WALSH, EDWARD**
- The Fairy Nurse — 91
- Battle of Credran — 116
- Ailleen the Huntress — 166
- Brighidin Ban-mo-Stor — 190

**WILLS, REV. J.:**
- The Burial — 73

# ADVERTISEMENT.

"THE BOOK OF IRISH BALLADS" is intended as a sequel to "THE BALLAD POETRY OF IRELAND." I trust it will not be found unworthy of taking its place beside that volume. It has been my most anxious wish that this collection of native ballads should be altogether divested of a sectarian or party complexion, and that every class of which THE IRISH NATION is composed should be poetically represented therein. Should there be, in those ballads which admit of the introduction of religious or political sentiment, a preponderance of one kind over another, the inequality is to be attributed to the abundance or scantiness of my materials—and not to any prejudice or bias of my own. I trust that the classification which I have made will be found correct and useful. In all but the Historical Ballads, I have endeavoured to arrange them with as much variety as possible; in that division they are placed in chronological order. As I have stated at the conclusion of my introduction, I have endeavoured to make this volume as original as possible; and I have therefore avoided, as much as I could, collections which had been previously made. It is for this reason that I have not included any of the poems of my lamented and revered friend, THOMAS DAVIS,—forming, as the public are aware, a separate volume of "The Library of Ireland."

# INTRODUCTION.

It has been said, by a well-known authority, that the Ballads of a people are more influential than their laws, and perhaps he might have added, more valuable than their annals. The most comprehensive survey that the eye of genius can take in—the most ponderous folio that ever owed its existence to the united efforts of industry and dulness, must fail in giving a perfect idea of the character of a people, unless it be based upon the revelations they themselves have made, or the confessions they have uttered. Without these, history is indeed but the "old almanack" that an illustrious countryman of ours\* has called it; a mere dry dead catalogue of dates and facts, useless either as a picture of the past, or as a lesson for the future. A people of passionate impulses, of throbbing affections, of dauntless heroism, will invariably not only have done things worthy of being recorded, but will also have recorded them. Myriads of human beings cannot be moved about noiselessly, like an army of shadows. The sullen sound of their advancing will be heard afar off; and those who see them not, will listen to the shrill music of their fifes and the merry echoes of their bugles. The great heavings of a people's heart, and, from time to time, the necessary purifying of the social atmosphere, will make themselves felt and heard and seen, so that all men may

\* Lord Plunkett

take cognizance thereof—as the mighty waves of the roused ocean dash against each other with a war-cry, or as the electric spirit proclaimeth its salutary mission in a voice of thunder.

In almost all countries the BALLAD has been the instrument by which the triumphs, the joys, or the sorrows of a people have been proclaimed.

Its uses have been numerous; its capabilities are boundless.

Long ago, in the fresh youth and enthusiasm of the world, how harmonious were its modulations—its revelations how divine! Then it sang of gods and heroes, and the milk-expanded warm breasts of the beneficent mother; and the gift of Ceres, aud the olive of Minerva, and the purple clusters of the son of Semele. Then it was, that, "standing on a pleasant lea," men could

> "Have glimpses that would make them less forlorn,
> Have sight of Proteus rising from the sea,
> Or hear old Triton blow his wreathed horn."*

Then it was that the earth was truly peopled. Neither was the air void, nor were the waters desolate. Shapes of beauty —

> "Schöne†

wandered familiarly with men; and nymphs and shepherds, and fauns and hamadryads, danced together beneath the eye of Jove himself in the shadow of blue Olympus, or beside the Venus-bearing foam of the sparkling isle-surrounding Hellespont. Had not poetry preserved this memory of the golden age—had not Hesiod and Homer built their beautiful and majestic structures on the original ballads that were probably floating among the people,—how dark, and gloomy, and indistinct would be our ideas of the old world: What visions that have been delighting the eye of man these three thousand years would have been lost: Of

---

\* Wordsworth.
† "Lovely beings from the Fable-land."—SCHILLER.

what examples of devotion, of heroism, of love of country, would the sincere and zealous of all nations have been deprived.

Poetry, after all, is the only indestructible gift that genius can bequeath to the world. The shield of Achilles, though the work of a god, has disappeared from the world, but the bounding words in which it has been described are immortal. This very shield itself, as Schiller remarks, is the type of the poet's mind, and of all true poetry.\* On it, we are told, were figured, not only representations of cities, implements of husbandry, corn fields and vineyards, sheep and oxen, and other things adapted to particular localities, and which may vary under different circumstances,—but the great fabricator had also introduced representations of the unchangeable wonders of creation, which are the same yesterday, to-day, and to-morrow,—

"For in it he represented earth—in it the sea and sky,—
In it the never wearied sun—the moon, exactly round;
And all those stars with which the brows of ample heaven are crown'd!" †

Thus a genuine poem must be true not only to the character of the age in which it is written, but in accordance with the principles of nature and of truth, which are unchangeable.

The Latins, a people very different from the Greeks, added but little to the beauty of the mythology they borrowed, or to the literature they imitated. With the exception of Egeria,—"a beautiful thought, and softly bodied forth,"—there are none of their native divinities that interest us much. Their early history, so full of stern, unbending justice, self-denial and heroism, is

\* "As the god and the genius, whose birth was of Jove,
   In one type all creation reveal'd,
   When the ocean, the earth, and the star-realm above,
   Lay compress'd in the orb of a shield,—
   So the poet, a shape and a type of the All,
   From a sound, that is mute in a moment, can call!"
[From "The Four Ages of the World."—Bulwer's Translation

† Iliad. Book xviii., Chapman's Translation.

considered either allegorical or wholly fabulous, and founded upon the memory of rude ballads, which had ceased to exist even at the time when their earliest annals were written.* In their latter years, the lyrics of Horace redeemed the character of their literature from the reproach of servile imitation; and some of these, and a few of the shorter tales of Ovid, are the only poems they have left us partaking, however remotely, of the character of Ballad Poetry, but much closer to the modern than to the ancient Homeric standard.— After this there is no trace of the ballad spirit in Latin literature. Its writers became more servile and less vigorous in their imitation, until, in the reign of Theodosius, the race of old Roman poets became extinct in the person of Claudian.

While this lamentable but natural decline of intellectual vigour, consequent upon the effeminacy and excesses of Imperial Rome, was developing itself along the sunny shores of the Mediterranean, a new order of things was maturing amid the mountains and forests of northern and western Europe. The human mind—which, in these remote regions, like their wintry seas, had been perpetually frozen—now began to melt and dissolve into brilliancy and activity. Those who lived upon the stormy shores of the ocean followed the sea-kings in their adventurous expeditions among the islands. Those who lived amid the dark forests of the interior, marched in search of brighter skies and more fruitful plains, towards the genial regions of the south. And it was in these expeditions, particularly the former, that the Bards of the Sea Kings gave the Ballad its modern shape and character. The sagas composed by them, to commemorate the triumphs or to bewail the disasters of their chiefs in "Icy Ierne"—the Scottish islands and Iceland—strongly resemble, both in structure and design, the more vigorous of the modern ballads. A new

---

* Mr. Macaulay's "Lays and Legends of Ancient Rome" are founded on this supposition. I am glad that I have this opportunity of expressing my admiration of these splendid and vigorous ballads, and of the other writings of their gifted and accomplished author.

race of divinities and a new race of heroes superseded the old classical models. Thor and Wodin succeeded Mars and the son of Priam, and, like the songs in which they were commemorated, what they lost in interest and beauty was compensated for by vigour and durability. The black and chilly waters of the northern seas were not a fitting birth-place for the Aphrodisian Venus; instead of the queen of love and gladness, the mighty kraken and the winged dragon were their children, who in many a stormy ballad have played their fearful and important parts ever since.

Again, in the sunny South, but not in exhausted Italy, did the harmony of song arise. Spain, that magnificent country, combining together the grandeur and the beauty of the North and the South—the bold mountains and caverned shores of Norway, and the enchanting graces of Parthenope—had already, even in the most palmy days of Latin literature, contributed some of the most boasted names to the catalogue of Roman writers. Lucan, who sang of Pharsalia; the two Senecas, the younger of whom is the only Roman tragic writer who has come down to us; and Martial, whose wit and licentiousness at once enlivened and disgraced the reign of Domitian—were natives of Spain; the three former of Carduba, and the latter of Arragon. But it was in the eighth century that the splendour and interest of Spanish history commences. In that century the Saracens conquered Spain, and introduced into it, along with a knowledge of letters and the sciences superior to what was possessed by any other people then in Europe, all the splendour and imagination of Oriental poetry. About the end of the twelfth century the celebrated poem of "The Cid" was written, commemorating the valorous exploits and adventures of the hero, Rodrigo de Bivar. Since that period, Spain has been pre-eminently rich in ballad poetry. Its grand, sonorous language, so musical as to have earned the epithet of "the poetry of speech," has been employed to good purpose; and nobler ballads than the Spanish, in praise of heroism, of virtue, of piety, and of love, the world has never seen. The capabilities of the Ballad have there been put to the severest test. Those of the heroic class, which detail the struggles of the old Spaniards with the Goth or with the Saracen, like Chevy Chase, "stir the heart as if with a trumpet;" while the sighing of a summer breeze in Andalusia is not more soft and gentle than the harmony of the passionate ballads that to this day are sung beneath the curtained balconies of moon-lit Sevilla. Garcilasso, Lopé, Calderon, Cervantes—great names are these, of which Spain and human nature may be proud.

The Ballad Poetry of England and Scotland has been very copious and very excellent for several centuries; and the Ballads of each contrast not so much in merit as in character. In the Song, which may be called the very essence and spirit of the Ballad, or the musical utterance of feeling and passion in the very paroxysm of their presence, Scotland has immeasurably the superiority. In that Pythian moment, when the mind is in its state of utmost activity, and the dominancy of passion is supreme, the concentrated expression of both is Song; and its appearance and the frequency of its return depend principally upon the character and constitution of each people. The Ballad, on the contrary, requires not the same degree of excitement,—Narrative, which is almost an essential portion of it, being incompatible with that mental and sensuous excitation which gives both to the song, and which is but momentary in its abiding. And thus the different success of the two, in the different nations of Europe, is as marked and distinct as the races of which they are composed. In Italy and France, in Scotland and Ireland—all nations sprung from the one family—the Song has been cultivated with the greatest success; whereas in the northern nations, in Germany and in England, the natural expression of the poetical instincts of the people has been through the calmer and more lengthened channel of the Ballad. Spain has succeeded better in both, perhaps, than any other nation;—the dominion of the Goths leaving after it much of the solemnity of thought and feeling of the Germanic races,—while the lyric capabilities of the language are such as to render the expression of high-wrought sentiment easy and obvious. In England the ballads are generally of a quiet and pastoral beauty— quite in character with the rural and sylvan charms of its scenery. The Robin Hood ballads, which so delight us in boyhood, and which give us visions of "Merry Sherwood".—

> In summer time, when leaves grow green,
> And birds sing on every tree,

that we never forget, and which are only replaced by the still more exquisite glimpses that Shakspeare opens to us of The Forest of Ardennes—all partake of this character—in them there is many a merry trick played, and many a mad adventure—

> "Of brave little Jonn,
> Of Fryer Tuck and Will Scarlet,
> Loxley, and Maid Marion."

Bold Robin and Allin-a-Dale, or the "Jolly Tanner," Arthur-a-Bland, have many a good contest with stout quarter-staffs—right merry to read and well described— but the writers scarcely ever forget, even for a few stanzas, the beauty of the summer woods where their heroes dwell, and satisfy their own hearts, and will delight their readers for all time, by this frequent recurrence to the unchangeable and everlasting delights of nature. Indeed, this continued reference to the beauty of the external world, which we meet in the old English poets, particularly in Chaucer (whose pictures of many a "May Morn-ing" are still so fresh after many years), may be the reason that they are read even now, notwithstanding the difficulties of an antiquated and obsolete dialect.

The Scotch Ballads are less numerous and less varied than the English; but in point of perfection—in the particular class, at least, of sentiment and the affections—they are not only superior to these, but, as I humbly conceive, to any Ballads that have ever been written. Their simplicity never degenerates into bold commonplace, nor their homeliness into vulgarity; and they are as far removed from maudlin sentimentality in their passionate heartiness, as from frigid conceits and prettinesses in their illustrations. The very heart of the Scottish people bounds in their ballads; we can listen to the ever-varying changes of its pulsation—now heavy and slow as the tides of Loch Lomond—now rapid and bounding as the billows of the Clyde. The "bonny blue e'en" of the lassie glance through her waving hair like a stream through the overhanging heather; and her arch reply or her merry laugh rings on our ears like the song of the mavis or the throssil. The ballads of a few of her humblest children have rendered Scotland dear to the hearts of all whose affections are worth possessing: they have converted (to the mind at least) her desolate heaths and barren mountains, into smiling gardens and olive-bearing hills; and have constructed among mists and storms, and the howling of the lashed Northern Ocean, an Arcadia dearer than that of yore, where "the shepherd's boy piped as though he should never be old."* Although my space here is very limited, I cannot refrain from presenting, to some of my readers perhaps for the first time, a specimen of these Ballads, taken almost at random, in support of what I have asserted, and as a model (in connexion with those written in a kindred spirit by some of our own countrymen—Griffin, Callanan, Davis, and Mr. Ferguson) of this most exquisite department of Ballad Poetry:—

### MARY OF CASTLE-CARY.†

Saw ye my wee thing, saw ye my ain thing,
 Saw ye my true love down on yon lea—
Crossed she the meadow yestreen at the gloaming,
 Sought she the burnie where flowers the haw-tree?
Her hair it is lint-white, her skin it is milk-white,
 Dark is the blue of her soft rolling e'e;
Red, red are her ripe lips, and sweeter than roses,
 Where could my wee thing wander frae me?

I saw nae your wee thing, I saw nae your ain thing,
 Nor saw I your true love down by yon lea;
But I met my bonnie thing late in the gloaming,
 Down by the burnie where flowers the haw-tree.

\* Sir Philip Sidney.
† Written by Hector MacNeill;

Her hair it was lint-white, her skin it was milk-white,
 Dark was the blue of her soft rolling e'e;
Red, red were her ripe lips, and sweeter than roses,
 Sweet were the kisses that she gave to me.

It was nae my wee thing, it was nae my ain thing,
 It was nae my true love ye met by the tree;
Proud is her leal heart, and modest her nature,
 She never loved ony till ance she loved me.
Her name it is Mary—she's frae Castle-Cary,
 Aft has she sat when a bairn on my knee;
Fair as your face is, were't fifty times fairer,
 Young bragger, she ne'er wad gie kisses to thee.

It was then your Mary; she's frae Castle-Cary
 It was then your true love I met by the tree
Proud as her heart is, and modest her nature,
 Sweet were the kisses that she gave to me.
Sair gloomed his dark brow, blood red his cheek grew,
 Wild flashed the fire frae his red rolling e'e;
Ye'se rue sair this morning your boasts and your scorning,
 Defend ye, fause traitor, fu' loudly ye lie.

Away wi' beguiling, cried the youth, smiling—
 Off went the bonnet. the lint white locks flee.
The belted plaid fa'ing, her white bosom shawing,
 Fair stood the loved maid wi' the dark rolling e'e.
Is it my wee thing, is it my ain thing,
 Is it my true love here that I see ?
O Jamie, forgi'e me, your heart's constant to me,
 I'll never mair wander, dear laddie, frae thee.

The most modern, and perhaps the most important class of ballads, remains to be alluded to—namely, the German. The sudden awakening, the rapid maturity, the enduring vitality, and the acknowledged supremacy of German literature, are facts as wonderful as they are consoling. Little better than a century ago, with the exception of a few theological and historical writers, the Germans were more destitute of a native literature, and were more dependant on other countries, particularly France, for intellectual supplies, than we have ever been; and now their works crowd the book markets of the world. Little more than a century ago a great German prince, called Frederick, a philosopher and a patron of philosophers, pronounced his native language but fit for horses,—little dreaming of the angels and angelic women—of the Katherines, the Theklas, and the Undines—from whose inspired lips that rough, nervous language would flow so harmoniously that all men would listen to the melody thereof. In no intellectual field have the Germans of the past and present centuries been defeated. Their drama is superior to any other that has appeared in Europe during the same period—for I presume there can be no comparison between the Shaksperian power of Schiller and the soft graces of Metestatio or even the more masculine classicalities of Alfieri Their histories are the mines in which even the most industrious writers search for the precious ore of truth. Their philosophy has been either a beacon or an *ignis fatuus* to the inquiring intellects of Europe; while some of their artists have come off victorious even in the Eternal Metropolis of art itself. In every department of literature German intellect has been renewing the almost exhausted fountains of the world. Like the Egyptian river, the great German Rhine has been overflowing the earth, and fruits, and flowers, and waving corn are springing luxuriantly in all lands. In the ballad the Germans have pre-eminently succeeded. It is with them somewhat of a short epic, in which the romance and chivalry of the middle ages find a suitable vehicle for their illustration. They seldom treat of humble life and simple passion, like the Scotch; or individual heroism, like the Spanish. They are more historical and legendary than directly sentimental or heroic; but through all runs a vein of philosophical abstraction and thoughtful melancholy, which imparts to them a peculiar and enduring charm. There is scarcely an historical event of any importance—a legend possessing the slightest interest—a superstition, not destitute of grace, sublimity, or terror—a river or a mountain that has anything to recommend it, that has not found an illustrator, an admirer, and a laureate among the German Balladists. And the consequence is, that not only is the German intellect honoured and respected, but the German land is also strengthened and enriched. The separate though confederated nations of Germany have been bound together as one people, by the universal language of their poetry;* and year after year pilgrims and students from strange lands wander thither, not attracted so much by the gloom of her woody mountains and the magic windings of her Rhine, as because (thanks to poetry) through the former the wild Jager still hunts and the witches dance on Walpurgis † nights, and because the latter has been made the crystal barrier of a free people, and the emblem, in its depth, its strength, and its beauty, of the German character and intellect.

It only remains for me to advert to what has been done, and what I conceive may be done, in Ireland with the ballad. If we recollect the constant state of warfare—the revolution upon revolution—the political struggles, and the generally unhappy condition of the people ever since the invasion, it is matter of surprise that there could be found any persons with hearts or intellects sufficiently strong to escape from the realities around them into the abstractions and idealities of poetry; but that there were many who did so, and with a power and beauty for which they get little credit, must be evident from Mr. Duffy's "Ballad Poetry," and, I trust, also from this volume. I speak now, of course, of our native Irish writers. To us there can scarcely be anything more interesting or more valuable than these snatches and fragments of old songs and ballads, which are chapters of a nation's autobiography. Without these how difficult would it be for the best disposed and the most patriotic amongst us to free our minds from the false impressions which the study (superficial as it was) of the history of our country, as told by those who were not her children or her friends, had made upon us. Instead of the rude savage kerns that anti-Irish historians represent our forefathers to have been, for ever hovering

* " Where'er resounds the German tongue—
Where German hymns to God are sung—
There, gallant brother, take thy stand!
That is the German's Fatherland!"
 [Mangan's " Anthologia Germanica," vol. ii., p. 180.]
† Walpurgis is the name of a saint to whom the first of May is dedicated.

with murderous intent round the fortresses of the Pale, we see them, in their own ballads, away in their green vallies and inaccessible mountains, as fathers, as brothers, as lovers, and as husbands, leading the old patriarchal life with their wives and children, while the air is musical with the melody of their harps and the lowing of their cattle;—we see them hunting the red deer over the brown mountains, or spearing the salmon in the pleasant rivers,—or, borne on their swift horses, descending in many a gallant foray on the startled intruders of the Pale. What is of more importance, we look into the hearts and minds of these people—we see what they love with such passion—what they hate with such intensity—what they revere with such sacred fidelity. We find they had love—they had loyalty—they had religion—they had constancy—they had an undying devotion for the "green hills of holy Ireland," and as such they are entitled to our respect, our affections, and our imitation. The best ballads they have left us are those of the affections, and they are, according to Mr. Ferguson, of the utmost possible intensity of passion, compatible with the most perfect purity. Even in their political ballads, where a thin disguise was necessary, the allegory has been so perfect, and the wail of sorrow, or the yearning of affection, so exquisitely imitated, (as in the instance of the *Roisin Dhu*, or "Dark Rosaleen,") as to make so excellent a critic and so true a poet as Mr. Ferguson doubt if they be in reality political ballads at all.

Upon the subject of our Anglo-Irish Ballads, I have nothing to add to what Mr. Duffy has so ably and so truly written in his introduction to the "Ballad Poetry of Ireland." That there is a distinct character and a peculiar charm in the best ballads of this class which the highest genius, unaccompanied by thorough Irish feeling, and a thorough Irish education, would fail to impart to them,—must be evident to every one who has read that volume. To those among us, and to the generations who are yet to be among us, whose mother tongue is, and of necessity must be, the English and not the Irish, the establishing of this fact is of the utmost importance, and of the greatest consolation:—that we can be thoroughly Irish in our writings without ceasing to be English; that we can be faithful to the land of our birth, without being ungrateful to that literature which has been "the nursing mother of our minds," that we can develop the intellectual resources of our country, and establish for ourselves a distinct and separate existence in the world of letters, without depriving ourselves of the advantages of the widely-diffused and genius-consecrated language of England, are facts that I conceive cannot be too widely disseminated. This peculiar character of our poetry is, however, not easily imparted. An Irish word or an Irish phrase, even appositely introduced, will not be sufficient; it must pervade the entire poem, and must be seen and felt in the construction, the sentiment, and the expression. Our writers would do well to consider the advantages, even in point of success and popularity, which would be likely to attend the working of this peculiar vein of Anglo-Irish literature. If they write, as they are too much in the habit of doing, in the weak, worn-out style of the majority of cotemporary English authors, they will infallibly be lost in the crowd of easy writers and smooth versifiers, whose name is legion, on the other side of the channel; whereas, if they endeavour to be racy of their native soil, use their native idiom, illustrate the character of their country, treasure her legends, eternalize her traditions, people her scenery, and ennoble her superstitions, the very novelty will attract attention and secure success. *

In conclusion I have only to state that I have endeavoured to draw the materials of this volume as much as

---

* No one can doubt the truth of this, who regards the state of the nterary world in England at present. Every native topic and every native mode of authorship seem so thoroughly exhausted (or, to use the expressive cant phrase, so completely "used up") that we find the great London book merchants drawing from Sweden and Denmark, from Iceland, from Russia, and the far East, some temporary supply for the literary wants of the day. This, of course, is not the motive that should influence our writers; but the suggestion in this age may not be without its use.

possible from hitherto unused sources. It was my original intention to have extracted copiously from the quarto edition of "The Spirit of the Nation," as it contains many exquisite ballads, by Mr. Duffy, Mr. Williams, Mr. Barry, Mr. Lane, Mr. Drennan, and other writers, which have never been published in any very cheap or very accessible form. I found, however, the number of poems which were still even newer to the public than those, so abundant, that I have confined myself to the selection of two from that work—one of them ('The Muster of the North)* principally because I believe it to be the best historical ballad the country has yet produced; and the other, as illustrating the most remarkable period of political excitement within my own memory. I have to regret that this volume does not contain a greater number of the poems of our greatest Poet—THOMAS MOORE. I would have been proud to have testified my admiration of him as a Poet and a Man, by extracting largely from his works—as, to my mind, many of his songs are perfect ballads—as faultless in design as they are exquisitely conceived and executed. In publishing these ballads, however, I considered I would be but giving most of my readers what they have already possessed, so that in reality no one suffers by the omissions but myself, a very humble but a very willing victim to the unbounded popularity of THOMAS MOORE.

I blush to allude to myself, so soon after such a name, but I fear I owe some apology to the reader for the introduction into this collection of three of my own poems—"the wish of friends" in this, as in so many other instances, has of course prevailed.

D. F. M'CARTHY.

28, Upper Baggot-street,
September, 1846.

---

* By an accident "The Muster of the North" is placed among the Political instead of the Historical Ballads.

# BOOK OF IRISH BALLADS.

## BALLADS

### ILLUSTRATIVE OF THE FAIRY MYTHOLOGY AND TRADITIONS OF IRELAND.

### A FAIRY TALE.

#### BY THOMAS PARNELL.

[I have been induced to retain this Ballad of Parnell, notwithstanding its unmistakable English dress—to some extent for the simple grace and beauty of its style—but principally because the story, however disguised, is essentially Irish, and illustrates very pleasingly some of the pranks and mingled benevolence and malice of "the good people." There is scarcely a child in the country, old enough to have its imagination or its taste for the marvellous developed, that is not familiar with some version of this story, learned in many instances where Parnell himself first heard it, in an Irish nurse's arms. This he confesses in the stanza of the ballad which precedes the last. Parnell, in imitating the old English style—in placing the scene of his poem "in Britain's Isle and Arthur's days"—(Spenser, so skilled in all the chronology and topography of fairy land, had already settled the question of time and place), and in adding a new flower to the already beautiful fairy garland of England. was actuated I believe by no conscious dislike for his native country; but his doing so was quite in keeping with the habits of his life. For being, as Goldsmith informs us, alwaye "very much elated or depressed, and his whole life spent in agony or rapture," he invariably gave his English friends the benefit of his rapture and elation; but when the gloomy fit returned, he would fly back to Ireland, and vent his spleen and agony in satirical songs, on the scenery and people that surrounded him. These songs I believe have not been preserved, at least they are not given in any edition of his works that I have seen. Goldsmith was a great admirer of the "Fairy Tale," and pronounced it, notwithstanding its defective imitation of the old dialect, as "incontestibly one of the finest pieces in any language."

The most accessible Irish version of the story, and I believe the most popular, is that which is given in Crofton Croker's "Fairy Legends of Ireland," where "Lusmore" acts the part of "Edwin," and "Jack Madden" that of the luckless "Sir Topaz."]

In Britain's isle, and Arthur's days,
When midnight fairies danc'd the maze,
    Liv'd Edwin of the Green;
Edwin, I wis, a gentle youth,
Endow'd with courage, sense, and truth,
    Though badly shap'd he'd been.

His mountain back mote well be said,
To measure height against his head,
    And lift itself above;
Yet, spite of all that nature did
To make his uncouth form forbid,
    This creature dar'd to love.

He felt the charms of Edith's eyes,
Nor wanted hope to gain the prize,
    Could ladies look within;
But one Sir Topaz dress'd with art,
And, if a shape could win a heart,
    He had a shape to win.

Edwin, if right I read my song,
With slighted passion pac'd along
    All in the moony light;
'Twas near an old enchanted court,
Where sportive fairies made resort
    To revel out the night.

His heart was drear, his hope was cross'd,
'Twas late, 'twas far, the path was lost
    He reach'd the neighbour town;
With weary steps he quits the shades,
Resolv'd, the darkling dome he treads,
    And drops his limbs adown.

But scant he lays him on the floor,
When hollow winds remove the door,
    And trembling rocks the ground;
And well I ween to count aright,
At once a hundred tapers light
    On all the walls around.

Now sounding tongues assail his ear,
Now sounding feet approachen near,
    And now the sounds increase:
And from the corner where he lay
He sees a train profusely gay
    Come prankling o'er the place.

But (trust me, gentles!) never yet
Was dight a masquing half so neat,
    Or half so rich before;
The country lent the sweet perfumes,
The sea the pearl, the sky the plumes,
    The town its silken store.

Now whilst he gaz'd, a gallant drest
In flaunting robes above the rest,
    With awful accent cry'd:
"What mortal of a wretched mind,
Whose sighs infect the balmy wind,
    Has here presum'd to hide?"

At this the swain, whose vent'rous soul
No fears of magic art control,
    Advanc'd in open sight;
"Nor have I cause of dread," he said,
"Who view, by no presumption led,
    Your revels of the night.

"'Twas grief, for scorn of faithful love,
Which made my steps unweeting rove
    Amid the nightly drew."
"'Tis well," the gallant cries again,
"We fairies never injure men
    Who dare to tell us true.

"Exalt thy love-dejected heart,
Be mine the task, or ere we part,
   To make thee grief resign;
Now take the pleasure of thy chaunce
Whilst I with Mab, my partner, daunce;
   Be little Mable thine."

He spoke, and all a sudden there
Light music floats in wanton air:
   The monarch leads the queen;
The rest their fairy partners found:
And Mable trimly tript the ground
   With Edwin of the Green.

The daucing past, the board was laid,
And siker such a feast was made,
   As heart and lip desire;
Withouten hands the dishes fly,
The glasses with a wish come nigh,
   And with a wish retire.

But now, to please the fairy king,
Full every deal they laugh and sing,
   And antic feats devise;
Some wind and tumble like an ape,
And other some transmute their shape
   In Edwin's wondering eyes.

Till one at last, that Robin hight,
Renown'd for pinching maids by night,
   Has bent him up aloof;
And full against the beam he flung,
Where by the back the youth he hung
   To sprawl uneath the roof.

From thence, "Reverse my charm," he cries,
"And let it fairly now suffice
   The gambol has been shown."
But Oberon answers with a smile,
"Content thee, Edwin, for a while,
   The vantage is thine own."

Here ended all the phantom-play;
They smelt the fresh approach of day,
    And heard a cock to crow;
The whirling wind that bore the crowd
Has clapp'd the door, and whistled loud,
    To warn them all to go.

Then screaming all at once they fly,
And all at once the tapers die:
    Poor Edwin falls to floor;
Forlorn his state, and dark the place,
Was never wight in such a case
    Through all the land before.

But soon as Dan Apollo rose,
Full jolly creature home he goes,
    He feels his back the less;
His honest tongue and steady mind
Had rid him of the lump behind,
    Which made him want success.

With lusty livelyhed he talks,
He seems a dancing as he walks,
    His story soon took wind;
And beauteous Edith sees the youth
Endow'd with courage, sense, and truth,
    Without a bunch behind.

The story told, Sir Topaz mov'd,
The youth of Edith erst approv'd.
    To see the revel scene.
At close of eve he leaves his home,
And wends to find the ruin'd dome
    All on the gloomy plain.

As there he bides, it so befel
The wind came rustling down a dell,
    A shaking seiz'd the wall;
Up spring the tapers as before,
The fairies bragly foot the floor,
    And music fills the hall.

But certes sorely sunk with woe
Sir Topaz sees the Elphin show,
    His spirits in him die:
When Oberon cries, "A man is near,
A mortal passion, cleeped fear,
    Hangs flagging in the sky."

With that Sir Topaz, hapless youth!
In accents faultering, ay for ruth,
    Intreats them pity grant:
For als he been a mister wight
Betrayed by wandering in the night
    To tread the circled haunt.

"A Losell vile," at once they roar,
"And little skill'd of fairy lore;
    Thy cause to come, we know;
Now has thy kestrel courage fell;
And fairies, since a lie you tell,
    Are free to work thee woe."

Then Will who bears the wispy fire
To trail the swains among the mire,
    The caitiff upwards flung;
There, like a tortoise in a shop,
He dangled from the chamber-top,
    Where whilome Edwin hung.

The revel now proceeds apace,
Deftly they frisk it o'er the place,
    They sit, they drink, and eat;
The time with frolic mirth beguile,
And poor Sir Topaz hangs the while
    Till all the rout retreat.

By this the stars began to wink,
They shriek, they fly, the tapers sink,
    And down y-drops the knight:
For never spell by fairy laid
With strong enchantment bound a glade,
    Beyond the length of night.

Chill, dark, alone, adreed, he lay,
Till up the welkin rose the day,
  Then deem'd the dole was o'er:
But wot ye well his harder lot?
His seely back the bunch had got
  Which Edwin lost afore.

This tale a Sybil-nurse ared;
She softly stroak'd my youngling head,
  And when the tale was done,
"Thus some are born, my son," she cries,
"With base impediments to rise,
  And some are born with none.

"But virtue can itself advance
To what the favourite fools of chance
  By fortune seem'd design'd;
Virtue can gain the odds of fate,
And from itself shake off the weight
  Upon th' unworthy mind."

---

## THE FAIRY WELL OF LAGNANAY.

### BY SAMUEL FERGUSON, M.R.I.A.

#### I.

Mournfully, sing mournfully—
 "O listen, Ellen, sister dear:
Is there no help at all for me,
 But only ceaseless sigh and tear?
 Why did not he who left me here,
With stolen hope steal memory?
 O listen, Ellen, sister dear,
(Mournfully, sing mournfully)—
 I'll go away to Sleamish hill,
I'll pluck the fairy hawthorn-tree,
 And let the spirits work their will;
 I care not if for good or ill,

So they but lay the memory
  Which all my heart is haunting still !
(Mournfully, sing mournfully)—
  The Fairies are a silent race,
And pale as lily flowers to see;
  I care not for a blanched face,
  Nor wandering in a dreaming place,
So I but banish memory:—
  I wish I were with Anna Grace!"
Mournfully, sing mournfully !

### II.

Hearken to my tale of woe—
  'Twas thus to weeping Ellen Con,
Her sister said in accents low,
  Her only sister, Una bawn :
'Twas in their bed before the dawn,
And Ellen answered sad and slow,—
  "Oh Una, Una, be not drawn
(Hearken to my tale of woe)—
  To this unholy grief I pray,
Which makes me sick at heart to know,
  And I will help you if I may :
—The Fairy Well of Lagnanay—
Lie nearer me, I tremble so,—
  Una, I've heard wise women say
(Hearken to my tale of woe )—
  That if before the dews arise.
True maiden in its icy flow
  With pure hand bathe her bosom thrice,
  Three lady-brackens pluck likewise,
And three times round the fountain go,
  She straight forgets her tears and sighs."
Hearken to my tale of woe !

### III.

All alas! and wellaway !
  " Oh, sister Ellen, sister sweet,
Come with me to the hill I pray,
  And I will prove that blessed feat !"
They rose with soft and silent feet,
They left their mother where she lay,

Their mother and her care discreet,
  (All, alas! and wellaway!)
And soon they reached the Fairy Well,
The mountain's eye, clear, cold, and grey,
  Wide open in the dreary fell:
How long they stood 'twere vain to tell,
At last upon the point of day,
  Bawn Una bares her bosom's swell,
  (All, alas! and wellaway)!
Thrice o'er her shrinking breasts she laves
The gliding glance that will not stay
  Of subtly-streaming fairy waves:—
And now the charm three brackens craves,
She plucks them in their fring'd array:—
  Now round the well her fate she braves,
  All alas! and wellaway!

### IV.

Save us all from Fairy thrall!
  Ellen sees her face the rim
Twice and thrice, and that is all—
  Fount and hill and maiden swim
  All together melting dim!
"Una! Una!" thou may'st call,
  Sister sad! but lith or limb
(Save us all from Fairy thrall!)
Never again of Una bawn
Where now she walks in dreamy hall,
  Shall eye of mortal look upon!
Oh! can it be the guard was gone,
That better guard than shield or wall?
  Who knows on earth save Jurlagh Daune?
(Save us all from Fairy thrall)!
Behold the banks are green and bare,
No pit is here wherein to fall:
  Aye—at the fount you well may stare,
  But nought save pebbles smooth is there,
And small straws twirling, one and all.
  Hie thee home, and be thy pray'r,
Save us all from Fairy thrall.

## HY-BRASAIL—THE ISLE OF THE BLEST.

### BY GERALD GRIFFIN.

["The people of Arran fancy that at certain periods they see *Hy-Brasail* elevated far to the west in their watery horizon This had been the universal tradition of the ancient Irish, who supposed that a great part of Ireland had been swallowed by the sea, and that the sunken part often rose, and was seen hanging in the horizon ! Such was the popular notion. The *Hy-Brasail* of the Irish is evidently a part of the *Atalantis* of Plato,* who, in his 'Timæus,' says that that island was totally swallowed up by a prodigious earthquake. Of some such shocks the isles of Arran, the promontories of Antrim, and some of the western islands of Scotland, bear evident marks."—*O'Flaherty's Sketch of the Island of Arran.*]

On the ocean that hollows the rocks where ye dwell,
A shadowy land has appeared, as they tell ;
Men thought it a region of sunshine and rest,
And they called it *Hy-Brasail*, the isle of the blest.
From year unto year, on the ocean's blue rim,
The beautiful spectre showed lovely and dim ;
The golden clouds curtained the deep where it lay,
And it looked like an Eden, away, far away !

A peasant who heard of the wonderful tale,
In the breeze of the Orient loosened his sail ;
From Ara, the holy, he turned to the west,
For though Ara was holy, *Hy-Brasail* was blest.
He heard not the voices that called from the shore—
He heard not the rising wind's menacing roar ;
Home, kindred, and safety, he left on that day,
And he sped to *Hy-Brasail*, away, far away !

Morn rose on the deep, and that shadowy isle,
O'er the faint rim of distance, reflected its smile ;
Noon burned on the wave, and that shadowy shore
Seemed lovely, distant, and faint as before ;
Lone evening came down on the wanderer's track,
And to Ara again he looked timidly back ;
Oh ! far on the verge of the ocean it lay,
Yet the isle of the blest was away, far away !

* For a ballad on this subject, by the Rev. G. Croly, see page 17.

Rash dreamer, return! O, ye winds of the main,
Bear him back to his own peaceful Ara again.
Rash fool! for a vision of fanciful bliss,
To barter thy calm life of labour and peace.
The warning of reason was spoken in vain;
He never re-visited Ara again!
Night fell on the deep, amidst tempest and spray,
And he died on the waters, away, far away!

---

## THE MOUNTAIN SPRITE.

#### BY THOMAS MOORE.

In yonder valley there dwelt, alone,
A youth, whose moments had calmly flown,
'Till spells came o'er him, and, day and night,
He was haunted and watch'd by a Mountain Sprite.

As once, by moonlight, he wander'd o'er
The golden sands of that island shore;
A foot-print sparkled before his sight—
'Twas the fairy foot of the Mountain Sprite!

Beside a fountain, one summer day,
As bending over the stream he lay,
There peeped down o'er him two eyes of light,
And he saw in that mirror the Mountain Sprite.

He turn'd, but, lo! like a startled bird,
That spirit fled!—and the youth but heard
Sweet music, such as marks the flight
Of some bird of song, from the Mountain Sprite.

One night, still haunted by that bright look,
The boy, bewilder'd, his pencil took;
And guided only by memory's light,
Drew the once-seen form of the Mountain Sprite.

"Oh, thou, who lovest the shadow," cried
A voice, low whispering by his side,
"Now turn and see"—here the youth's delight
Seal'd the rosy lips of the Mountain Sprite.

"Of all the spirits of land and sea,"
Then rapt he murmur'd, "there's none like thee;
And oft, oh oft, may thy foot thus light
In this lonely bower, sweet Mountain Sprite!"

---

## THE CITY OF GOLD.

[This is another ballad on the beautiful fable of a phantom island in the Atlantic.]

Years onward have swept,
  Aye! long ages have rolled—
Since the billows first slept
  O'er the City of Gold!

'Neath its eddy of white
  Where the green wave is swelling,
In their halls of delight
  Are the fairy tribes dwelling.

And, but seldom the eye
  Of a mortal may scan,
Where those palaces high
  Rise unaided by man.

Yet, at times the waves sever,
  And then you may view
The yellow walls ever
  'Neath the ocean's deep blue.

But I warn thee, O man!
  Never seek to behold,
Where the crystal streams run
  In the City of Gold!

Like a beauty with guile,
  When some young knight has found her,
There is death in her smile,
  And dark ruin around her!

Like a Poet's first dream,
  In his longings for glory;
A dagger whose gleam,
  With the life blood is gory.

Like wishes possessed,
  And for which we have panted,
When we find us unblest,
  Tho' our prayers have been granted.

Like ought that's forbidden,
  Weak man to behold,
Death and sorrow are hid in
  The City of Gold.

Rash youth! dost thou view it,
  The ransom thou'lt pay,
Alas! thou must rue it,
  Death takes thee to-day!

---

## Cobaṅ-ṅa-Sja,*

### OR,
## THE FAIRY WELL.

#### BY JAMES TEELING.

[Amongst the many old and fanciful superstitions embodied in the traditions of our peasantry, some of the most poetical are those connected with spring wells, which in Ireland have been invested with something of a sacred character ever since the days of Druidical worship. It is in some parts of the country an article of popular belief, that the desecration of a spring, by any unworthy use, is invariably followed by some misfortune to the offender; and that the well itself, which is regarded as the source of fruitfulness and prosperity, moves altogether out of the field in which the violation had been committed.—*Dub. University Mag.*, vol. viii., p. 447.]

Oh! Peggy Bawn was innocent,
  And wild as any roe;

    * Thubber-na-Shie.

Her cheek was like the summer rose,
　Her neck was like the snow;

And every eye was in her head
　So beautiful and bright.
You'd almost think they'd light her through
　Glencarrigy by night.

Among the hills and mountains,
　Above her mother's home,
The long and weary summer day
　Young Peggy Blake would roam;

And not a girl in the town
　From Dhua to Glenlur,
Could wander through the mountain's heath
　Or climb the rocks with her.

The Lammas sun was shinin' on
　The meadows all so brown;
The neighbours gathered far and near
　To cut the ripe crops down;

And pleasant was the mornin',
　And dewy was the dawn,
And gay and lightsome hearted
　To the sunny fields they're gone.

The joke was passing lightly,
　And the laugh was loud and free;
There was neither care nor trouble
　To disturb their hearty glee;

When, says Peggy, resting in among
　The sweet and scented hay,
"I wonder is there one would brave
　The Fairy-well to-day!"

She looked up with her laughin' eyes
　So soft, at Willy Rhu;
Och murdher! that she didn't heed
　His warnin' kind and true!

But all the boys and girls laughed,
   And Willy Rhu looked shy;
God help you, Willy! sure they seen
   The throuble in your eye.

"Now, by my faith!" young Connell says,
   "I like your notion well—
There's a power more than gospel
   In what crazy gossips tell."

Oh, my heavy hatred fall upon
   Young Connell of Sliabh-Mast!
He took the cruel vengeance
   For his scorned love at last.

The jokin' and the jibin',
   And the banterin' went on
One girl dared another,
   And they all dared Peggy Bawn.

Till leaping up, away she flew
   Down to the hollow green—
Her bright locks, floating in the wind,
   Like golden lights were seen.

They saw her at the Fairy well—
   Their laughin' died away,
They saw her stoop above its brink
   With heart as cold as clay.

Oh! mother, mother, never stand
   Upon your cabin floor!
You heard the cry that through your heart
   Will ring for evermore;

For when she came up from the well,
   No one could stand her look!
Her eye was wild—her cheek was pale—
   They saw her mind was shook:

And the gaze she cast around her
  Was so ghastly and so sad—
"O Christ preserve us!" shouted all,
  "Poor Peggy Blake's gone mad!"

The moon was up—the stars were out,
  And shining through the sky,
When young and old stood mourning round
  To see their darling die.

Poor Peggy from the death-bed rose—
  Her face was pale and cold,
And down about her shoulders hung
  The lovely locks of gold.

"All you that's here this night," she said,
  "Take warnin' by my fate,
Whoever braves the Fairies' wrath,
  Their sorrow comes too late."

The tear was startin' in her eye,
  She clasp'd her throbbin' head,
And when the sun next mornin' rose
  Poor Peggy Bawn lay dead.

## FAIRY REVELS.

The fairies are dancing by brake and bower,
For this in their land is the merriest hour.

Their steps are soft, and their robes are light,
And they trip it at ease in the clear moonlight.

Their queen is in youth and in beauty there,
And the daughters of earth are not half so fair.

Her glance is quick, and her eyes are bright,
But they glitter with wild and unearthly light.

Her brow is all calm, and her looks are kind,
But the look that she gives leaves but pain behind.

Her voice is soft, and her smiles are sweet,
But woe to thee who such smiles shall meet.

She will meet thee at dusk like a lady fair,
But go not, for danger awaits thee there.

She will take thee to ramble by grove and by glen,
And the friends of thy youth shall not know thee again.

## THE ENCHANTED ISLAND.

[The tradition in this beautiful little ballad is almost the same as that on which "The City of Gold," "Hy-Brasail," and other poems in this collection are founded, except in point of locality; the scene of the latter ballads being placed in the Atlantic, to the west of the Isles of Arran, while "the Enchanted Island" is supposed to be in the neighbourhood of Rathlin Island, off the north coast of the county Antrim. The name of the island, which has been spelled a different way by almost every writer on the subject, is supposed to be derived from *Ragh-erin*, or "the Fort of Erin," as its situation, commanding the Irish coast, might make it, not unaptly, be styled "the fortress of Ireland."—See *Leonard's Topographia Hibernica.*]

To Rathlin's Isle I chanced to sail,
  When summer breezes softly blew,
And there I heard so sweet a tale,
  That oft I wished it could be true.

They said, at eve, when rude winds sleep,
  And hushed is ev'ry turbid swell,
A mermaid rises from the deep,
  And sweetly tunes her magic shell.

And while she plays, rock, dell, and cave,
  In dying falls the sound retain,
As if some choral spirits gave
  Their aid to swell her witching strain.

Then summoned by that dulcet note,
  Uprising to th' admiring view,
A fairy island seems to float
  With tints of many a gorgeous hue.

And glittering fanes, and lofty towers,
  All on this fairy isle are seen;
And waving trees, and shady bowers,
  With more than mortal verdure green.

And as it moves, the western sky
  Glows with a thousand varying rays;
And the calm sea, tinged with each dye,
  Seems like a golden flood of blaze.

They also say, if earth or stone,
  From verdant Erin's hallowed land,
Were on this magic island thrown,
  For ever fixed, it then would stand.

But, when for this, some little boat
  In silence ventures from the shore—
The mermaid sinks—hushed is the note,
  The fairy isle is seen no more!

## THE FAIRY RATH OF LOCH INNIN.

### BY ALEXANDER HENRY.

[The wild steed mentioned in this ballad is, I presume, the Phooka, a species of being which, perhaps, more than any other in the Fairy Mythology of Ireland, is capable of poetic illustration; and yet, with the exception of this, I have not been able to meet with any modern poem in which it is described. When I wrote my own ballad of "Alice and Una" (which I have placed last in this division), I was not aware of the existence even of this one. It was to supply, however inadequately, a deficiency that appeared to me extraordinary, and with the hope of inducing some person more competent than myself to undertake the illustration of our neglected or vulgarised traditions, that that ballad was written. The Phooka is of the maligant class of fairy beings, and he is as wild and capricious in his character as he is changeable in his form. At one time an eagle or an ignis fatuus, at another a horse or a bull, while occasionally he figures as "two single animals rolled into one," exhibiting a compound of the calf and goat. When he assumes the form of a horse, his great object, according to a recent writer, seems to be "to obtain a rider, and then he is in his most malignant glory. Headlong he dashes through briar and brake, through flood and fell, over mountain, valley, moor, or river indiscriminately; up or down precipice is alike to him, provided he gratifies the malevolence that seems to inspire him. He bounds and flies over and beyond them, gratified by the distress, and utterly reckless and ruthless of the cries and danger and suffering of the luckless wight who bestrides him. As the "Tinna Geolane," or "Will-o-the-Wisp," he lures bnt to betray. Like the Hanoverian "Tuckbold" he deludes the night wanderer into a bog, and leads him to his destruction in a quagmire or pit. Macpherson's spirit of Loda is evidently founded on the tradition of the Phooka; and in the Finnian Tales he is repeatedly mentioned as the "Puka (gruagach, or hairy spirit) of the blue valley."—CROKER'S FAIRY LEGENDS— HALL'S IRELAND.]

THE fair was o'er, the moon was high,
  The badger purr'd, the bog-sprite shone ;
From the dark cairn the beanshie's cry
  Had told some favourite friend was gone ;
      The plover
      Flew over
    The dark dewy wood :
      Each rath-fay
      His path way
Row'd o'er the night flood.
Jack Finn now bid his friends good night,
  And staggered towards his woodland cot :
A wild, good hearted, cheery wight
  As e'er smok'd pipe, or drained a pot.
      Thro' rushes
      And bushes
  He whistled loud, to show
      The bog-sprite
      With red light
  He fear'd not as a foe.
But now he passed a lonely tower,
  Where once bright mirth and splendour shone ;
But now, with mirth, with pride and power,
  Its very name was nearly gone.

The Leprechauns beneath it dwelt,
Poor Jack now missed the beaten path,
And soon, poor wight! he trembling felt
What ' twas to pass a Fairy rath:
As o'er its hollow sounding sod
　His heavy step now loudly rang,
A tiny form before him trod,
　And thus with wildest accents sang:
　　　"When moonlight
　　　Near midnight
　　Tips the rock and waving wood:
　　　When moonlight
　　　Near midnight
　　Silvers o'er the sleeping flood:
　　　When yew-tops
　　　With dew-drops
　　Sparkle o'er deserted graves.
　　　'Tis then we fly
　　　Thro' welkin high,
　　Then we sail o'er yellow waves."
On his head he wore a round plum'd hat,
　Form'd of fur of the old black rat;
His scarlet coat and purple breeches
　Were finely sown by fairies' stitches.
His stockings were made of the fine white down
　That tufted the soft, bloated night-moth's breast;
And the green golden-crested wren's bright crown
　Was stolen by elfins to trim his light vest;
His steed was a wild-bounding bearded goat,
　Whose trappings were made of the sanguine skin
Of a dead man's wrist, on which he could float
　Thro' water or air, as the wing or fin:
His jack-boots were made of the bat's tann'd wings;
His spurs were the bright golden queen-bees' stings;
The whistle that headed his wild flax whip
Was reav'd from a cricket; his pigmy hip
Was girt with a well-tempered sharp, long blade
Which once darn'd the hose of some fair housemaid
Thus equipp'd, he gallopp'd o'er hill and mead,
And now to the Fairy Rath doth lead.

The Rath was nigh deep Innin's lake,
Well fenced with rock-pine bush and brake;
The brown-back'd rabbit o'er it fed,
And in its soft sand furrowed—
But there (the red-ray'd evening's sun
When down) the fowler's murd'rous gun
Was heard no more—for woe the wight
Would tread it 'neath the lone moonlight.
Beside it lay the dreamless bed
Of those forgotten—long since dead;
For from the tombstones o'er them cast
Their names were worn by winter's blast.
Howe'er it be, Jack Finn got there—
  The Fairy King surrounded stood,
Amidst the moon's reflected glare.
  Of polish'd blades upon the flood,
(Which calmly sleeping on the sand,
  Did scarcely move the floating weed,)
And thus address'd his list'ning band,
  And thus Jack Finn's sad fate decreed:—
      "That mortal wight,
      Who roves by night,
      To dare the sprite,
      Who rides the light
      Of moonbeams bright,
      Shall feel his might:
      For this, I say,
      Till break of day,
      Jack Finn so gay,
      For this shall pay,—
      Help, witches gray,
      Ope' graves——Obey!"
'Twas now the fearful magic spell
  Did strongly work against Jack Finn,
For all the dead began to yell,
  And death's heads on the tombs to grin;
The coffins rose from moving graves,
And burst their red-worm—shining staves,
And each from whole or crumbling shroud
Said, "Jack, good night." then slowly bow'd.

And in their dark graves yawning fell,
Order'd by fearful magic spell;
And now the troops of fairy-land,
Grown to Jack's size, before him stand;
Jack's joy was great to see the crowd;
  He caught their King's false proffered hand
Then to him love and friendship vow'd,
  And join'd the seeming peasant band.
But little reck'd their leader's horse
  Was once a goat or speckled cat;
His fears were for the grinning corse
  Half ate by worms or charnel rat.
He mounted quick a sloe-black steed,
Noted in fairy-land for speed,
And joyous bade the ghosts good night,
Then with the elfins wing'd his flight—
The signal given, away he flew
  O'er the gray weedy charnel wall,
"Poor luckless Jack," shrill cried the crew,
  "Be silent when the fairies call."
They leap the scented hawthorn hedge,
  And gallop thro' the wavy mead,
And thro' the black bog, flags and sedge,
  Poor Jack now guides his magic steed:
Now the tall lonely tower of Slane
Rises o'er the dark demesne,
Which by the distance seem'd to shroud
Its ruined head in russet cloud;
But soon the creeping ivy's seen,
To cloak its breast with moon-ray'd green;
And fir, and oak, and shining holly,
Bedeck this throne of melancholy;
And sighing, shade alike the head
Of prince or begger mouldered,
Who 'neath the silent village lie,
  Close fenc'd with pale mist-covered groves,
Where soaring goshawks proudly fly,
  Where prowling fox securely roves.
And now the lordly Castle's seen,
  As if the tower it sought to join,

With woody arms of dappled green,
  Reflected in the sullen Boyne.
Dark misty woods the distance cloud,
And black bent oaks the river crowd,
Save on those turns that smoothly shine,
Devoid of rocks, rough-crown'd with pine!
Reflected clouds with silver swell,
Here slowly pass, as if they fell
To kiss the stream and bid it flow
With joy—but hoarse with sallow woe
Has deep Boyne run, since Tara's Kings
Had with their blood imbrued its springs.
Jack, led by fairies—wretched wight!
  Was nearly dead thro' fright and woe,
And silent cursed the luckless night,
  And Fay, that caused his being so.
They quickly leap'd across the Boyne,
  Save Jack (who thought he now was free);
But soon his snorting horse did join
  With him the pigmy company.
Hark! hark! said one, I hear a flute,
List! list! my friends, be still and mute!
I see a boat, sure mortals breathe
That note upon the waves beneath—
The mellow horn, the flute and harp,
Are nearing now the gurgling sharp—
They silent pass, with dripping oars
Uplifted—now soft music pours,
Again—the barge's dipping wings,
Ruffle the stream with sparkling rings;
The swelling notes are passing near,
  Now beats in time the stroke of oars,
And on the moon-lit waves appear
  Their boiling rings, which lave the shores.
The sailing music echoes thro'
  Dark hanging woods—Boyne's canopy—
The castle turrets bound the view,
  The passing harp-chords softly sigh.
The boat now smoothly floats away,
Its oars are deck'd with yellow spray;
The notes are softer—now they die,

And could be drown'd by Jack's deep sigh.
But in his breast he breathless held
That heavy throb, until compell'd
  To sob it forth—the barge is fled,
  The listening night wind followed—
With trembling Jack, the fairies pranc'd
  O'er Bective, and o'er old Bellsoon;
In Creasetown's vale, round Jack they danc'd,
  Beneath the yellow setting moon.
Then towards the Shannon flew away,
And leap'd the Shannon every Fay.
But Jack, who thought it ne'er was in
A fiend or mortal horse's skin
To cross a full half mile of flood,
In the De'il's stirrups gazing stood.
But, hark! that distant whistle shrill
That's echoed from yon moon-lit hill;
Now hark! Jack's courser's answering neigh,
Now see him wheel with Jack away,
And like a swift ball from a cannon
Leap with poor Jack the river Shannon.
"Cuirle mo chroide,"\* said Jack, "you are.
Away flew steed like meteor star
With fiery tail, and shook poor Jack
Upon the bank from off his back.

---

## THE PHANTOM CITY.

### BY GERALD GRIFFIN.

A STORY I heard on the cliffs of the west,
  That oft, through the breakers dividing,
A city is seen on the ocean's wild breast
  In turreted majesty riding.
But brief is the glimpse of that phantom so bright,
  Soon close the white waters to screen it;
And the bodement, they say, of the wonderful sight,
  Is death to the eyes that have seen it.

\* Cushlamachree.

I said, when they told me the wonderful tale,
  My country, is this not thy story?
Thus oft through the breakers of discord we hail
  A promise of peace and of glory.
Soon gulphed in those waters of hatred again
  No longer our fancy can find it,
And woe to our hearts for the vision so vain,
  For ruin and death come behind it.

---

## THE MAGIC WELL.

#### A LEGEND OF KILLARNEY.

#### BY W. M. DOWNES.

[This ballad is founded upon the following legend:—" There was once upon a time, near the western coast of Ireland, a romantic valley inhabited by a few peasants, whose rude cabins were surrounded by the most luxuriant trees, and sheltered by mountains rising almost perpendicularly on every side. Ireland has still many beautiful green vales; but there is not one so deeply, so securely nestled among the hills, as the one of which I speak. Add the depth of the deepest of these lakes to the height of the loftiest mountain that towers above us, and you may then form some idea of the deep seclusion of this forgotten valley. Norah was the prettiest girl in the little village: she was the pride of her old father and mother, and the admiration of every youth who beheld her. There was but one spring of water in this valley; it was a little well of the brightest and clearest water ever seen, which bubbled up from the golden sand, and then lay calmly sleeping in a basin of the whitest marble. From this basin there did not appear to be any outlet; the water ran into it incessantly, but no one could detect that any part of it escaped again! It was a Fairy Well! There was a tradition concerning it which had, time out of mind, been handed down from parent to child. It was covered with a huge stone, which, though apparently very heavy, could be removed with ease by the hand of the most delicate female; and it was said to be the will of the fairy who presided over it, that all the young girls of the village should go thither every evening after sunset, remove the stone, and take from the marble basin as much water as would be sufficient for the use of each family during the ensuing day: above all, it was understood to be the fairy's strict injunction, that each young maiden, when she had filled her pitcher, should carefully replace the stone; for if at any time this were neglected, the careless maiden would not only bring ruin on herself, but likewise on all the inhabitants of the valley; and if the morning sun ever shone upon the water, inevitable destruction would follow." The remainder of the story is given in the Ballad.]

NEAR Erin's western coast, of yore,
  There was a deep romantic vale;
The loveliest on her island shore!
  So says the legendary tale.

And scatter'd on its verdant bed,
  A little rustic hamlet rose;
Where peasant swains sequester'd led
  A blissful life of calm repose.

O'erhung by mountains high and wild!
  And shaded 'midst a thick'ning wood;
Their lowly simple dwellings smil'd,
  In this secluded solitude.

Sweet gentle Norah was most fair:—
  Her father and her mother's pride!
And like a beauteous lily there
  She grew—and none her charms denied.

The cottage where her parents dwell'd,
  Surrounded by luxuriant green,
For rural neatness far excell'd
  All others in the village scene.

The honey-suckle's twining wreath,
  By Norah nurs'd—its walls array'd;
And sweet wild flowers bloom'd beneath,
  The culture of this artless maid.

Here was one well of waters bright,
  So pure that angels there might sip!
As clear as e'er met human sight,—
  Or ever cool'd a mortal lip.

In marble basin there it lay;
  Soft bubbling up from golden sands.
Whence came its source no tongue could say,
  Save from the power of fairy hands.

A voice of olden time declar'd—
  "Twas form'd by some unearthly spell,
And all within the vale rever'd
  This magic spring—"the fairy well."

Above it rose a shading stone,
  Which, though of pond'rous weight and size,
The gentlest female touch alone
  Its massive bulk with ease could rise.

Tradition pass'd from man to man,
  (Since time—from memory's page decay'd,)
That thus the fairy's mandate ran—
  Who o'er its crystal waters sway'd:

It was her firm command—and will,
  That none (till evening's ray had fled)
Should seek the well, or dare to fill
  Their pitchers from its magic bed.

But when the sunset's parting glow,
  In western skies no longer shone—
Then each young village girl could go—
  And, fearless, move the mystic stone.

One strict injunction, too, she gave,—
  That as each maiden fill'd her vase,
Before she turn'd the fount to leave,
  With caution should the stone replace.

For if the morning sunbeam play'd
  On the uncover'd limpid spring,
The folly of the careless maid
  Would ruin to the valley bring.

Full oft—with pitcher in her hand,
  And flow'rets in her raven hair;
Warbling the music of her land!
  Went Norah—tripping lightly there.

In innocence and beauty, both,
  To be belov'd—the maid was form'd!
And to the valley came a youth—
  Whose heart, her charms, her virtue warm'd.

A soldier he—in armour clad;
  One who, though young, had seen the world!
And often bared a warrior's blade,
  When warfare's banner was unfurl'd.

Oft with the stranger Norah walk'd—
  (In shady pathways wild and lone,)
And he of brighter regions talk'd,
  That rural life had never known.

But could there be a happier scene,
  Than in that lovely spot retir'd!
That blooming valley, ever green,
  With all that nature's wants requir'd.

With tales of love her heart he won!
  And when unto the well she hied,
(Soon as went down the setting sun,)
  Coolin was ever—at her side.

But when her parents found she lov'd
  This stranger youth—their wrath was sore;
Their child's attachment they reprov'd,
  And warn'd her ne'er to meet him more!

She wept, yet promis'd to obey;
  And when the cloud of evening fell,
In sadness went a diff'rent way,
  That led her to the fairy well.

And there she sate—the well beside,
  As o'er the vale the night-shade stole;
While bitterly the maiden cried—
  For saddening sorrow swell'd her soul!

From heaven's bright vault the moonlight's gleam
  Glanc'd downward on the fountain clear;
O'er Norah's cheek its radiance came—
  And chang'd to pearl her falling tear.

" Oh come not here—again to me,"
  (Exclaim'd the maid in sorrow deep!)
" Alas, why did I ever see
  One—who has taught me how to weep?"

" Ah dearest Norah! say not so;
  My love, my life are only thine!
Could I have caus'd thy tear to flow?
  Depart with me—nor thus repine."

The maid replied—" No! never—no!
  With thee I've promis'd not to meet:
But yet, where'er I turn or go,
  Still dost thou trace my wandering feet."

She rose—nor yet the tear was dried,
  That late stole down her pallid cheek;
Her cares to lull, the soldier tried,
  And soothingly began to speak.

Her hand the lover fondly grasp'd,
  Like one who felt a pang to part;
And then with warm affection clasp'd
  The maiden to his throbbing heart.

Now treading swift the beaten track,
  They left the well—that lonely spot!
Thus spoke the youth while pacing back
  With Norah to her father's cot:

"Thy parents will forgive," said he,
  "Our close attachment, when they know
The tender love I bear to thee;
  To me thy hand they will bestow!

"Thou could'st not leave for scenes more gay,
  Them, and thy native valley too:
Oh then, thy Coolin here shall stay!
  What would he not resign for you?

"Thy smile a desert's gloom would cheer
  And make it seem enchanting, bright;
And now, my love, thy home is near;
  Give me that smile, and so good night."

The maiden did as he requir'd;
  In hope of bliss, no more she wept.
Then softly to her couch retir'd,
  And wrapt in pleasing vision slept.

When lo—as from some frightful dream
  Of hideous fiends—or demons fell—
She started with a shrill wild scream!
  And loud exclaimed—"the well! the well!"

"I have not fix'd the shading stone,
  Perhaps as yet 'tis not too late;
The morning beam not yet hath shone!
  I'll haste—I'll run and know my fate."

Along the well-known path she flew,
  (With swiftness like a hunted roe:—)
The eastern hills rose on her view,
  And in the sun-rise seem'd to glow!

As one by magic power subdued—
  (Or by a spectral sight amaz'd)
At length—she like a statue stood,
  As downward on the well she gaz'd.

## IRISH BALLADS.

The bright unclouded morning ray
   Its light upon the spot hath cast.
The spring, that once so gentle lay,
   Was rushing now—a torrent vast!

Each moment wider o'er the vale
   Its fearful waters foaming spread:
As, with a wild and maniac wail,
   The peasants from the village fled.

But hapless Norah! void of fear,
   Still stood upon the hillock path;
Unconscious of her danger near,—
   She watch'd the flood in swelling wrath!

As fierce pour'd on the angry tide,
   Close to the maid her lover ran:
My parents save—oh haste"—she cried!
   "From thee my only woes began!"

She fell—he rais'd the prostrate fair,
   And bore her up a rising hill;
But the white torrent even there,—
   Deep, vengeful, rolling, followed still.

Swift round the wooded height it rose,
   Which lesser yet—and lesser grew;
And soon the refuge that they chose,
   Was sunk—and nearly lost to view!

"Oh, could we reach yon mountain's brow,"
   Poor Coolin to his Norah cries!
"But hope of life is vanish'd now;
   Behold, the fearful floods arise!

" Alas! sweet girl—my own dear love!
   This dismal fate could I foresee;—
Far from thee would I fly—nor prove
   The cause of thy dire destiny."

Unaw'd by death —no vain alarms
  The lovers felt—but watch'd their doom:
Clasp'd sadly in each other's arms,
  They glanc'd down on the surgy tomb!

Soon to their feet upsprung the flood,
  Its ruthless waters whelm'd them o'er;
The less'ning spot on which they stood
  Above the waves was seen no more!

Gone was the valley of the well:—
  The fairy's deed of wrath was done!
The foaming waters ceas'd to swell,
  And soft in tranquil calmness shone.

But never shall sweet Norah wake,—
  Or Coolin, from their slumber deep!
Now laid beneath Killarney's lake,
  The maiden and her lover sleep.

## ARRANMORE.

### BY THOMAS MOORE.

["The Inhabitants of Arranmore are still persuaded that in a clear day they can see from this coast Hy-Brasail, or the Enchanted Island, the Paradise of the Pagan Irish, and concerning which they relate a number of romantic stories."—*Beaufort's Ancient Topography of Ireland.*]

Oh! Arranmore, loved Arranmore,
  How oft I dream of thee;
And of those days when, by thy shore,
  I wander'd young and free.
Full many a path I've tried, since then,
  Through pleasure's flow'ry maze,
But ne'er could find the bliss again
  I felt in those sweet days.

How blithe upon thy breezy cliffs
  At sunny morn I've stood,
With heart as bounding as the skiffs
  That danced along thy flood ;
Or when the western wave grew bright
  With daylight's parting wing,
Have sought that Eden in its light,
  Which dreaming poets sing.

That Eden, where th' immortal brave
  Dwell in a land serene,—
Whose bowers beyond the shining wave,
  At sunset oft are seen ;
Ah, dream, too full of saddening truth !
Those mansions o'er the main
Are like the hopes I built in youth,
  As sunny and as vain !

---

## THE ISLAND OF ATLANTIS.

### BY THE REV. G. CROLY.

[" For at that time the Atlantic Sea was navigable, and had an island before that mouth which is called by you the pillars of Hercules. But this island was greater than both Libya and all Asia together, and afforded an easy passage to other neighbouring islands, as it was easy to pass from those islands to all the Continent which borders on this Atlantic Sea. * * * But, in succeeding times, prodigious earthquakes and deluges taking place, and bringing with them desolation in the space of one day and night, all that warlike race of Athenians was at once merged under the earth; and the Atlantic island itself being absorbed in the sea, entirely disappeared."—*Plato's Timæus.*]

Oh ! thou Atlantic, dark and deep,
  Thou wilderness of waves,
Where all the tribes of earth might sleep
  In their uncrowded graves !

The sunbeams on thy bosom wake,
  Yet never light thy gloom ;
The tempests burst, yet never shake
  Thy depths, thou mighty tomb !

Thou thing of mystery, stern and drear,
  Thy secrets who hath told?—..
The warrior and his sword are there,
  The merchant and his gold.

There lie their myriads in thy pall.
  Secure from steel and storm;
And he, the feaster on them all,
  The canker-worm.

Yet on this wave the mountain's brow
  Once glow'd in morning's beam;
And, like an arrow from the bow,
  Out sprang the stream:

And on its bank the olive grove,
  And the peach's luxury,
And the damask rose—the nightbird's love—
  Perfumed the sky.

Where art thou, proud Atlantis, now?
  Where are thy bright and brave?
Priest, people, warriors' living flow?
  Look on that wave!

Crime deepen'd on the recreant land,
  Long guilty, long forgiven;
There power uprear'd the bloody band,
  There scoff'd at Heaven.

The word went forth—the word of woe—
  The judgment-thunders pealed;
The fiery earthquake blazed below;
  Its doom was seal'd.

Now on its halls of ivory
  Lie giant weed and ocean slime,
Burying from man's and angel's eye
  The land of crime.

## THE HAUNTED SPRING.

#### BY SAMUEL LOVER.

[It is said, Fays have the power to assume various shapes for the purpose of luring mortals into Fairyland; hunters seem to have been particularly the objects of the lady fairies' fancies.]

Gaily through the mountain glen
  The hunter's horn did ring,
    As the milk-white doe
    Escaped his bow,
Down by the haunted spring.
In vain his silver horn he wound,—
  'Twas echo answer'd back;
For neither groom nor baying hound
  Were on the hunter's track;
In vain he sought the milk-white doe
That made him stray, and 'scaped his bow.
For, save himself, no living thing
Was by the silent haunted spring.

The purple heath-bells, blooming fair,
Their fragrance round did fling,
    As the hunter lay
    At close of day,
Down by the haunted spring.
A lady fair, in robe of white,
  To greet the hunter came;
She kiss'd a cup with jewels bright,
  And pledged him by his name;
" Oh, lady fair," the hunter cried,
" Be thou my love, my blooming bride,
" A bride that well might grace a king!
" Fair lady of the haunted spring."

In the fountain clear she stoop'd,
  And forth she drew a ring;
    And that loved Knight
    His faith did plight
Down by the haunted spring.

But since that day his chase did stray,
   The hunter ne'er was seen,
And legends tell, he now doth dwell
   Within the hills so green;*
But still the milk-white doe appears,
And wakes the peasants' evening fears,
While distant bugles faintly ring
Around the lonely haunted spring.

---

## ALICE AND UNA.

### A TALE OF "Ceim-an-eic."†

#### BY D. F. M'CARTHY.

[The pass of Céim-an-eich (the path of the deer) lies to the south-west of Inchageela, in the direction of Bantry Bay. The tourist will commit a grievous error if he omit to visit it. Perhaps in no part of the kingdom is there to be found a place so utterly desolate and gloomy. A mountain has been divided by some convulsion of nature; and the narrow pass, about two miles in length, is overhung on either side by perpendicular masses clothed in wild ivy and underwood, with, occasionally, a stunted yew tree or arbutus growing among them. At every step advance seems impossible—some huge rock jutting out into the path; and, on sweeping round it, seeming to conduct only to some barrier still more insurmountable; while from all sides rush down the "wild fountains," and, forming for themselves a rugged channel, make their way onward—the first tributary offering to the gentle and fruitful Lee:

    "Here, amidst heaps
Of mountain wrecks, on either side thrown high,
The wide-spread traces of its watery might,
The tortuous channel wound."

Nowhere has nature assumed a more appalling aspect, or manifested a more stern resolve to dwell in her own loneliness and grandeur undisturbed by any living thing; for even the birds seem to shun a solitude so awful, and the hum of bee or chirp of grasshopper is never heard within its precincts.—*Hall's Ireland*, vol. i., p. 117.]

AH ! the pleasant days have vanished, ere our wretched
   doubtings banished

---

\* Fays and fairies, are supposed to have their dwelling places within old green hills.

† Céim-an-eich (the path of the deer).

All the graceful spirit people, children of the earth and
  sea—
They whom often, in the olden time, when earth was
  fresh and golden,
Every mortal could behold in haunted tower, and flower,
  and tree—
They have vanished, they are banished—ah! how sad the
  loss for thee,
    Lonely Céim-an-eich!

Still some scenes are yet enchanted by the charms that
  Nature granted,
Still are peopled, still are haunted by a graceful spirit
  band.
Peace and Beauty have their dwelling where the infant
  streams are welling—
Where the mournful waves are knelling on Glengariff's
  coral strand;*
Or where, on Killarney's mountains, Grace and Terr r
  smiling stand,
    Like sisters, hand in hand!

Still we have a new romance in fire-ships, through the
  tamed seas glancing,
And the snorting and the prancing of the mighty engine
  steed;
Still, Astolpho-like, we wander through the boundless
  azure yonder,
Realizing what seemed fonder than the magic tales we
  read—
Tales of wild Arabian wonder, where the fancy all is
  freed—
    Wilder far, indeed!

Now that Time, with womb unfolded, shakes the palsy
  from her old head,
Cries, "Oh! Earth, thou hast no soul dead, but a livi..
  soul hast thou!"

* In the bay of Glengariff, and towards the N.W. parts of Bantry
Bay, they dredge up large quantities of coral sand.—SMITH'S Cork
vol. i., p. 286.

Could we—could we only see all, blended with the lost
    Ideal,
These the glories of the Real, happy were the old world
    now—
Woman in its fond believing—man with iron arm and
    brow—
        Faith and Work its vow!

Yes! the Past shines clear and pleasant, and there's
    glory in the Present;
And the Future, like a crescent, lights the deepening
    sky of Time;
And that sky will yet grow brighter, if the Worker and
    and the Writer
Err not—as they surely might err—but unite in bonds
    sublime,
With two glories shining o'er them, up the coming years
    they'll climb
        Earth's great evening as its prime!

With a sigh for what is fading, but, oh! earth, with no
    upbraiding,
For we feel that time is braiding newer, fresher flowers
    for thee—
We will speak, despite our grieving, words of Loving
    and Believing,
Tales we vowed when we were leaving awful Céim-an-
    eich—
Where the sever'd rocks resemble fragments of a frozen
    sea,
        And the wild deer flee!

•        •        •        •

'Tis the hour when flowers are shrinking, when the
    weary sun is sinking,
And his thirsty steeds are drinking in the cooling Wes-
    tern sea;
When young Maurice lightly goeth, where the tiny
    streamlet floweth.

And the struggling moonlight showeth where his path
    must be—
Path whereon the wild goats wander fearlessly and free
    Through dark Céim-an-eich.

As a hunter, danger daring, with his dogs the brown
    moss sharing,
Little thinking, little caring, long a wayward youth lived
    he;
But his bounding heart was regal, and he looked as looks
    the eagle,
And he flew as flies the beagle, who the panting stag
    doth see—
Love, who spares a fellow-archer, long had let him wan-
    der free
        Through wild Céim-an-eich !

But at length the hour drew nigher when his heart
    should feel that fire ;
Up the mountain high and higher had he hunted from
    the dawn ;
Till the weeping fawn descended, where the earth and
    ocean blended,
And with hope its slow way wended to a little grassy
    lawn—
It is safe, for gentle Alice to her saving breast hath
    drawn
        Her almost sister fawn.

Alice was a chieftain's daughter, and, though many
    suitors sought her,
She so loved Glengariff's water that she let her lovers
    pine ;
Her eye was beauty's palace, and her cheek an ivory
    chalice,
Through which the blood of Alice gleamed soft as rosiest
    wine,
And her lips like lusmore blossoms which the fairies
    intertwine, †
        And her heart a golden mine.

† The lusmore (or fairy cap)—literally, the great herb.—*Digitalis Purpurea.*

She was gentler and shyer than the sweet fawn that
    stood by her,
And her eyes emit a fire soft and tender as her soul;
Love's dewy light doth drown her, and the braided locks
    that crown her
Than autumn's trees are browner, when the golden sha-
    dows roll
Through the forests in the evening, when cathedral tur-
    rets toll,
      And the purple sun advanceth to its goal.

Her cottage was a dwelling all regal homes excelling,
But, ah! beyond the telling was the beauty round it
    spread—
The wave and sunshine playing, like sisters each array-
    ing—
Far down the sea-plants swaying upon their coral bed
As languid as the tresses on a sleeping maiden's head,
      When the summer breeze is dead.

Need we say that Maurice loved her, and that no blush
    reproved her
When her throbbing bosom moved her to give the heart
    she gave;
That by dawn-light and by twilight, and oh! blessed
    moon, by thy light—
When the twinkling stars on high light the wanderer
    o'er the wave—
His steps unconscious led him where Glengariff's waters
    lave
      Each mossy bank and cave.

He thitherward is wending—o'er the vale is night de-
    scending—
Quick his step, but quicker sending his herald thoughts
    before;
By rocks and streams before him, proud and hopeful on
    he bore him;
One star was shining o'er him—in his heart of hearts
    two more—
And two other eyes, far brighter than a human head
    e're wore,
      Unseen were shining o'er.

These eyes are not of woman—no brightness merely human
Could, planet-like, illumine the place in which they shone;
But nature's bright works vary—there are beings, light and airy,
Whom mortal lips call fairy, and Una she is one—
Sweet sisters of the moonbeams and daughters of the sun,
    Who along the curling cool waves run.

As summer lightning dances amid the heavens' expanses,
Thus shone the burning glances, of those flashing fairy eyes;
Three splendours there were shining—three passions intertwining—
Despair and hope combining their deep contrasted dyes,
With jealousy's green lustre, as troubled ocean vies
    With the blue of summer skies!

She was a fairy creature, of heavenly form and feature—
Not Venus' self could teach her a newer, sweeter grace—
Not Venus' self could lend her an eye so dark and tender,
Half softness and half splendour, as lit her lily face;
And, as the stars' sweet motion maketh music throughout space,
    There was music in her face.

But when at times she started, and her blushing lips were parted,
And a pearly lustre darted from her teeth so ivory white
You'd think you saw the gliding of two rosy clouds dividing,
And the crescent they were hiding gleam forth upon your sight—
Through these lips, as through the portals of a heaven pure and bright,
    Came a breathing of delight!

She had seen young Maurice lately walk forth so proud
    and stately,
And tenderly and greatly she loved him from that hour;
Unseen she roamed beside him, to guard him and to
    guide him,
But now she must divide him from her human rival's
    power.
Ah! Alice—gentle Alice! the storm begins to lower
    That may crush Glengariff's flower!

The moon that late was gleaming, as calm as childhood's
    dreaming,
Is hid, and, wildly screaming, the stormy winds arise;
And the clouds flee quick and faster before their sullen
    master,
And the shadows of disaster are falling from the skies—
Strange sights and sounds are rising—but Maurice be
    thou wise,
    Nor heed the tempting cries.

If ever mortal needed that council, surely *he* did;
But the wile has now succeeded—he wanders from his
    path—
The cloud its lightning sendeth, and its bolt the stout oak
    rendeth,
And the firm arbutus bendeth in the whirlwind, as a
    lath!
Now and then the moon looks out, but, alas! its pale
    face hath
    A dreadful look of wrath.

In vain his strength he squanders—at each step he
    wider wanders—
Now he pauses—now he ponders where his present path
    may lead;
And, as he round is gazing, he sees—a sight amazing!—
Beneath him, calmly grazing, a noble jet-black steed.
"Now, Heaven be praised!" cried Maurice, "this is
    fortunate indeed—
    From this labyrinth I'm freed!"

Upon its back he leapeth, but a shudder through him
   creepeth,
As the mighty monster sweepeth like a torrent through
   the dell ;
His mane, so softly flowing, is now a meteor blowing,
And his burning eyes are glowing with the light of an
   inward hell—
And the red breath of his nostrils, like steam where the
   lightning fell,
      And his hoofs have a thunder knell !


What words have we for painting the momentary fainting
That the rider's heart is tainting, as decay doth taint a
   corse ?
But who will stoop to chiding, in a fancied courage
   priding,
When we know that he is riding the fearful Phooka
   Horse ?\*
Ah! his heart beats quick and faster than the smitings
   of remorse
      As he sweepeth through the wild grass and
      gorse !


As the avalanch comes crashing, 'mid the scattered
   streamlets splashing,
Thus backward wildly dashing, flew the horse through
   Céim-an-eich—
Through that glen so wild and narrow, back he darted
   like an arrow—
Round, round by Gougane Barra, and the fountains of
   the Lee,
O'er the "giant's grave" he leapeth, and he seems to
   own in fee
      The mountains and the rivers and the sea !

---

\* For a description of the Phooka, see Introduction to "The Fairy
Rath of Loch Innin," p. 42.

From his flashing hoofs who *shall* lock the eagle home
    of Malloc.\*
When he bounds, as bounds the Mialloch † in its wild
    and murmuring tide?
But as winter leadeth Flora, or the night leads on
    Aurora,
Or as shines green Glashenglora ‡ along the black
    hill's side—
Thus, beside that demon monster, white and gentle as a
    bride,
        A tender fawn is seen to glide.


It is the fawn that fled him, and that late to Alice led
    him—
But now it does not dread him, as it feigned to do
    before,
When down the mounting gliding, in that sheltered
    meadow hiding—
It left his heart abiding by wild Glengariff's shore—
For it was a gentle Fairy who the fawn's light form
    wore,
        And who watched sweet Alice o'er.


But the steed is backward prancing where late it was
    advancing,
And his flashing eyes are glancing, like the sun upon
    Loch Foyle—
The hardest granite crushing, through the thickest bram-
    bles brushing—
Now like a shadow rushing up the sides of Slieve-na-
    goil ! §

---

\* "Wildly from Malloc the eagles are screaming."—CALLANAN'S GOUGANE BARRA.

† Mialloch, "the murmuring river" at Glengariff.—SMITH'S CORK.

‡ Glashenglora, a mountain torrent, which finds its way into the Atlantic Ocean through Glengariff, in the west of the county of Cork. The name, literally translated, signifies "the noisy green water."—BARRY'S SONGS OF IRELAND, p. 173.

§ The most remarkable and beautiful mountain at Glengariff is the noble conical one whose ancient name is *Sliabh-na-goil* ("the mountain

And the fawn beside him gliding o'er the rough and
    broken soil,
        Without fear and without toil.

Through woods, the sweet birds' leaf home, he rusheth
    to the sea foam—
Long, long the fairies' chief home, when the summer
    nights are cool,
And the blue sea like a Syren, with its waves the steed
    environ,
Which hiss like furnace iron when plunged within a
    pool,
Then along among the islands where the water nymphs
    bear rule,
        Through the bay to Adragool.

Now he rises o'er Bearhaven, where he hangeth like a
    raven—
Ah! Maurice, though no craven, how terrible for thee?
To see the misty shading of the mighty mountains
    fading,
And thy winged fire-steed wading through the clouds
    as through a sea!
Now he feels the earth beneath him—he is loosen'd—
    he is free,
        And asleep in Céim-an-eich.

Away the wild steed leapeth, while his rider calmly
    sleepeth
Beneath a rock which keepeth the entrance to the glen,
Which standeth like a castle, where are dwelling lord
    and vassal,
Where within are wine and wassail, and without are
    warrior men—

of the wild people.") The miserable, unimaginative epithet of "Sugar Loaf" has here, as elsewhere, disgracefully usurped the fine old musical names which our ancestors gave to their hills. It is to be hoped that the people, if they have ears, not to talk of affections, recollections, or imagination, will get rid of their "Sugar Loaves" (which, they may be sure, were made in a "slave market") as soon as possible, and call their mountains by the names their fathers gave them.

But save the sleeping Maurice, this castle cliff had
   then
         No mortal denizen !*

Now Maurice is awaking, for the solid earth is shaking,
And a sunny light is breaking through the slowly opening stone—
And a fair page at the portal, crieth " Welcome, welcome! mortal,
" Leave thy world (at best a short ill), for the pleasant
   world we own—
" There are joys by thee untasted, there are glories yet
   unknown—
         " Come kneel at Una's throne."

With a sullen sound of thunder, the great rock falls
   asunder,
He looks around in wonder, and with ravishment awhile—
For the air his sense is chaining, with as exquisite a
   paining,
As when summer clouds are raining o'er a flowery Indian isle—
And the faces that surround him, oh! how exquisite
   their smile,
         So free of mortal care and guile.

These forms, oh! they are finer—these faces are diviner
Than Phidias even thine are, with all thy magic art;
For beyond a lover's guessing, and beyond a bard's ex-
   pressing,
Is the face that truth is dressing with the feelings of the
   heart ;
Two worlds are there together—Earth and Heaven have
   each a part—
         And such, divinest Una, thou art!

* There is a great square rock, literally resembling the description
of the text, which stands near the Glengariff entrance to the pass of
Kim-an eich.

And then the dazzling lustre of the hall in which they muster—
Where brightest diamonds cluster on the flashing walls around ;
And the flying and advancing, and the sighing and the glancing,
And the music and the dancing on the flower-inwoven ground,
And the laughing and the feasting, and the quaffing and the sound,
    In which their voices all are drowned.

But the murmur now is hushing—there's a pushing and a rushing,
There's a crowding and a crushing, through that golden, fairy place,
Where a snowy veil is lifting, like the slow and silent shifting
Of a shining vapour drifting across the moon's pale face—
For there sits gentle Una, fairest queen of fairy race,
    In her beauty, and her majesty, and grace.

The moon by stars attended, on her pearly throne ascended,
Is not more purely splendid than this fairy-girted queen ;
And when her lips had spoken, 'mid the charmed silence broken,
You'd think you had awoken in some bright Elysian scene ;
For her voice than the lark's was sweeter, that sings in joy between
    The heavens and the meadows green.

But her cheeks—ah ! what are roses ? What are clouds where eve reposes ?
What are hues that dawn discloses ? to the blushes spreading there ;
And what the sparkling motion of a star within the ocean,

To the crystal soft emotion that her lustrous dark eyes
    wear?
And the tresses of a moonless and a starless night are
    fair
        To the blackness of her raven hair.


"Ah! Mortal, hearts have panted for what to thee is
    granted—
To see the halls enchanted of the spirit world revealed;
And yet no glimpse assuages the feverish doubt that
    rages
In the hearts of bards and sages wherewith they may be
    healed;
For this have pilgrims wandered—for this have votaries
    kneeled—
        For this, too, has blood bedewed the field.


' And now that thou beholdest, what the wisest and the
    oldest,
What the bravest and the boldest, have never yet de
    scried—
Wilt thou come and share our being, be a part of what
    thou'rt seeing,
And flee, as we are fleeing, through the boundless ether
    wide?
Or along the silver ocean, or down deep where pearls
    hide?
        And I, who am a queen, will be thy bride.


" As an essence thou wilt enter the world's mysterious
    centre"—
And then the fairy bent her, imploring to the youth—
" Thou'lt be free of death's cold ghastness, and, with a
    comet's fastness,
Thou can'st wander through the vastness to the Para-
    dise of Truth,
Each day a new joy bringing, which will never leave,
    in south,
        The slightest stain of weariness and ruth."

As he listened to the speaker, his heart grew weak and
    weaker—
Ah! memory go seek her, that maiden by the wave,
Who with terror and amazement is looking from her
    casement,
Where the billows at the basement of her nestled cottage
    rave
At the moon, which struggles onward through the tem-
    pest, like the brave,
        And which sinks within the clouds as in a
        grave.


All maidens will abhor us—and it's very painful for
    us
To tell how faithless Maurice forgot his plighted vow;
He thinks not of the breaking of the heart he late was
    seeking—
He but listens to her speaking, and but gazes on her
    brow—
And his heart has all consented, and his lips are ready
    now
        With the awful, and irrevocable vow.


While the word is there abiding, lo! the crowd is now
    dividing,
And, with sweet and gentle gliding, in before him came
    a fawn;
It was the same that fled him, and that seemed so much
    to dread him,
When it down in triumph led him to Glengariff's grassy
    lawn,
When, from rock to rock descending, to sweet Alice he
    was drawn,
        As through Céim-an-eich he hunted from
        the dawn.


The magic chain is broken—no fairy vow is spoken—
From his trance he hath awoken, and once again is free;

And gone is Una's palace, and vain the wild steed's
  malice,
And again to gentle Alice down he wends through
  Céim-an-eich:
The moon is calmly shining 'over mountain, stream,
  and tree,
         And the yellow sea-plants glisten through
         the sea.

\* \* \* \*

The sun his gold is flinging, the happy birds are singing,
And bells are gaily ringing along Glengariff's sea;
And crowds in many a galley to the happy marriage
  rally
Of the maiden of the valley and the youth of Céim-an-
  eich;
Old eyes with joy are weeping, as all ask, on bended
  knee,
         A blessing, gentle Alice, upon thee!

# BALLADS

## ILLUSTRATIVE OF THE SUPERSTITIONS AND CUSTOMS OF IRELAND.

### THE FETCH.

**BY JOHN BANIM.**

[In Ireland, a Fetch is the supernatural *fac simile* of some individual, which comes to insure to its original, a happy longevity, or immediate dissolution. If seen in the morning, the one event is predicted; if in the evening, the other.—BANIM.]

THE mother died when the child was born,
    And left me her baby to keep;
I rocked its cradle the night and morn,
    Or, silent, hung o'er it to weep.

'Twas a sickly child through its infancy,
    Its cheeks were so ashy pale;
Till it broke from my arms to walk in glee,
    Out in the sharp, fresh gale.

And then my little girl grew strong,
    And laughed the hours away;
Or sung me the merry lark's mountain song,
    Which he taught her at break of day.

When she wreathed her hair in thicket bowers,
  With the hedge-rose and hare-bell blue,
I called her my May, in her crown of flowers,
  And her smile so soft and new.

And the rose, I thought, never shamed her cheek,
  But rosy and rosier made it;
And her eye of blue did more brightly break,
  Through the bluebell that strove to shade it.

One evening I left her asleep in her smiles,
  And walked through the mountains lonely;
I was far from my darling, ah! many long miles,
  And I thought of her, and her only!

She darkened my path, like a troubled dream,
  In that solitude far and drear;
I spoke to my child! but she did not seem
  To hearken with human ear.

She only looked with a dead, dead eye,
  And a wan, wan cheek of sorrow:
I knew her Fetch!—she was called to die,
  And she died upon the morrow.

---

## An Beanrıʒe.*

[The superstition of the Beanrıʒe is well known. It is believed to be an unearthly attendant on certain ancient families in this country,† and it is only seen or heard previous to the decease of some of its members. It appears in a variety of shapes, but usually as a small and beautiful woman, who, with a peculiarly mournful cry, bewails the misfortune about to fall upon the family she loves.]

FAIR EVELEEN sat in her tower high,
  On a calm and silent night;

---

\* The Banshee

† "For the high Milesian race alone
  Ever flows the music of her woe."
                              MANGAN.

And she gazed on the twinkling lamps of the sky,
  Than her own blue eyes less bright.


And the silver moonbeams bathed her brow,
  But her cheek was as cold and pale:
"Dearmidh's fleet foot is loitering now—
  Ah! whence is that dreadful wail!"


For wofully sad was the thrilling strain,
  Now borne upon the breeze;
And it fell on her brain like an icy chain,
  And her heart's blood began to freeze.


And still as the dying pauses swept,
  In their wailing sounds of fear,
The sobs and the plaints of one that wept
  Rose sadly upon her ear.


It was the Beanṛíʒe! and she came to tell
  A tale of sorrow and death;
For Dearmidh that night 'neath a rival fell,
  Upon *Moin-mor's\** dreary heath.


"Such unearthly sounds!" poor Eveleen well
  Their meaning could discover,
For soon the morning sunbeams fell
  On her corse, beside her lover!


    \* The great bog.

## CUSHEEN LOO.

### TRANSLATED FROM THE IRISH.

### BY J. J. CALLANAN.

[This song is supposed to have been sung by a young bride, who was forcibly detained in one of those forts which are so common in Ireland, and to which the good people are very fond of resorting. Under pretence of hushing her child to rest, she retired to the outer margin of the fort, and addressed the burthen of her song to a young woman whom she saw at a short distance, and whom she requested to inform her husband of her condition, and to desire him to bring the steel knife to dissolve the enchantment.]

SLEEP my child! for the rustling trees
Stirr'd by the breath of summer breeze,
And fairy songs of sweetest note,
Around us gently float.

Sleep! for the weeping flowers have shed
Their fragrant tears upon thy head,
The voice of love hath sooth'd thy rest,
And thy pillow is a mother's breast.
     Sleep my child!

Weary hath pass'd the time forlorn,
Since to your mansion I was borne,
Tho' bright the feast of its airy halls,
And the voice of mirth resounds from its walls.
     Sleep my child!

Full many a maid and blooming bride
Within that splendid dome abide,—
And many a hoar and shrivell'd sage,
And many a matron bow'd with age.
     Sleep my child!

Oh! thou who hearest this song of fear,
To the mourner's home these tidings bear.
Bid him bring the knife of the magic blade,
At whose lightning flash the charm will fade.
    Sleep my child!

Haste! for to-morrow's sun will see
The hateful spell renewed for me;
Nor can I from that home depart,
'Till life shall leave my withering heart.
    Sleep my child!

Sleep my child! for the rustling trees,
Stirr'd by the breath of summer breeze,
And fairy songs of sweetest note,
Around us gently float.

---

## THE BURIAL.

### BY THE REV. JAMES WILLS.

A FAINT breeze is playing with flowers on the hill,
The blue vault of summer is cloudless and still;
And the vale with the wild bloom of nature is gay,
But the far hills are breathing a sorrowful lay!

As winds on the *Clairseach's* sad chords when they
 stream,
As the voice of the dead on the mourner's dark dream!
Far away, far away, from gray distance it breaks,
First known to the breast by the sadness it wakes!

Now lower, now louder, and longer it mourns
Now faintly it falls, and now fitful returns;
Now near, and now nearer, it swells on the ear,
The wild *ululúa*, the death song is near!

With slow steps, sad burthen, and wild uttered wail.
Maid, matron, and cotter wind up from the vale;
And loud lamentations salute the gray hill,
Where their fathers are sleeping, the silent and still!

Wild, wildly that wail ringeth back on the air,
From that lone place of tombs, as if spirits were there,
O'er the silent, the still, and the cold they deplore, –
They weep for the tearless, whose sorrows are o'er.

## THE O'NEILL.

[Since this ballad was written, all necessary light has been thrown upon the character and exploits of AODH O'NEILL, by Mr. Mitchel in his most admirable and fearless life of that prince. To some of my readers, however, the original explanation given by the author of the ballad (in the Belfast Magazine) may be useful, and I therefore retain it with some abridgment. It is to the latter part of the tradition alluded to, that this poem owes its origin. " Hugh O'Neill, representative and chief of the powerful family of that name, in the year 1587, accepted of a patent from Queen Elizabeth, creating him Earl of Tir-owen; in the eyes of his kinsmen and followers this acceptance was an act of submission, and the title itself a degradation; The O'Neill being a royal name, and conferring on its holder kingly authority. The mark of favour bestowed by Elizabeth, was held by the Earl until 1595, in the spring of which year he suddenly called an assembly of the chiefs of his country, formally renounced the act of submission, and resumed the original distinguishing appellation of his forefathers—The O'Neill. The cause of this alteration in his conduct has been variously accounted for; but an old tradition, which is still current in the country where he flourished, attributes it wholly to the interference of a supernatural agent. After relating in a simple style what is stated above, it tells that for three nights previous to the calling of the assembly, the Banshee, or guardian spirit of the family, was heard in his castle of Dungannon, upbraiding him with his submission, conjuring him to throw off the odious epithet with which his enemies had branded him, rousing him to a sense of his danger by describing the sufferings of some of the neighbouring chiefs, charging him to arm, and promising him assistance."]

"CAN ought of glory or renown,
 "To thee from Saxon titles spring?
"Thy name a kingdom and a crown,
 "Tir-owen's chieftain, Ulster's king!"

These were the sounds that on the ear
   Of Tir-owen's startled Earl arose,
That blanch'd his alter'd cheek with fear,
   And from his pillow chas'd repose.

In vain was clos'd his weary eye,
   In vain his prayer for peaceful sleep,
Still from a viewless spirit nigh,
   Broke forth, in accents loud and deep:

" Can ought of glory or renown,
   " To thee from Saxon titles spring?
" Thy name a kingdom and a crown,
   " 'Tir-owen's chieftain, Ulster's king!

" Oft did thy eager youthful ear
   " Bend to the tale of Thomond's shame, *
" And, in thy pride of blood didst swear
   " To hold with life thy glorious name!

" Yet thou didst leave thy native land,
   " For honours on a foreign shore,
" And for submission's purchas'd brand,
   " Barter'd the name thy fathers bore!

" Where are those fathers' glories gone?
   " The pride of ages that have been!
" While tamely bows their traitor son,
   " The vassal of a Saxon queen:

" While still within a dungeon's walls,
   " Ardmira's fetter'd prince reclines, †
" While I'Maoile for her chieftain calls, ‡
   " Who in a distant prison pines:

---

* In the reign of Henry the Eighth, the palace of Cluan-road, near Ennis, in the county of Clare the magnificent, mansion of the chief of the O'Briens, was burned to the ground by those of his own blood, in revenge for his having accepted of the comparatively degrading title of Earl of Thomond.

† O Dogherty of Ardmir, who was seized and thrown into prison by the lord deputy Fitzwilliam.

‡ O'Toole of I'Maoile, father to the wife of O'Neill, also imprisoned by Fitzwilliam.

While from that corse, yet reeking warm,
" O'er his own fields the life-streams flow,
" Well mayst thou start! that mangled form
" Once was thy friend, Mac Mahon Roe. *

" Forget'st thou that a vessel came
" To Cineal's strand, in gaudy pride,
" Fraught with each store of valued name,
" That nature gave or art supplied :

No voice to bid the youth beware,
" Of banquets by the Saxon spread ;
' He tasted, and the treacherous snare
" Clos'd o'er the young O'Donnell's head. †

Hopeless, desponding, still he lies,
" No aid his griefs to soothe or end ;
" And oft in vain his languid eyes
" Turn bright'ning on his father's friend :

" Who was that friend ?—a chief of power,
" The guardian of a kingdom's weal,
Tir-owen's pride and Ulster's flower,
" A prince, a hero, THE O'NEILL !

" He, at whose war-horn's potent blast,
" Twice twenty chiefs in battle tried,
" Unsheath'd the sword in warlike haste,
" And rang'd their thousands on his side.

" But now he dreads the paths to tread,
" That lead to honours, power, and fame ;
" And stands, each nobler feeling dead,
" Nameless, who own'd a monarch's name.

---

* Hugh Roe Mac Mahon, chief of Monaghan, who was tried before Fitzwilliam, by a jury of common soldiers, and butchered at his castle door.

† O'Donnell, son of the chief of Tyrconnell, who was decoyed on board a vessel and carried prisoner to Dublin, where he was detained from his fourteenth until his twentieth year, when he made a desperate effort to escape, and succes lost.

"Shall Ardmir's prince for ever groan,
　"And I'Maoile's chief still fetter'd lie?
"None for Mac Mahon's blood atone?
　"Nought cheer O'Donnell's languid eye?

"To thee they turn, on thee they rest:
　"Release the chain'd, revenge the dead,
"Or soon the halls thy sires possest,
　"Shall echo to a stranger's tread!

"And in the sacred chair of stone, *
　"The base Ne Gaveloc † shalt thou see
"Receive the name, the power, the throne,
　"That once was dear as life to thee!

"Arise! for on his native plains
　"His father's warriors marshall'd round,—
"O'Donnell, freed from Saxon chains,
　"Shall soon the signal trumpet sound:

"And soon, thy sacred cause to aid,
　"The brave O'Cahan, ‡ at thy call,
"Shall brandish high the flaming blade,
　"That filled the grasp of Cuie-na-gall:

"Resume thy name, in arms arise,
　"Tear from thy breast the Saxon star,
"And let the coming midnight skies
　"Be crimson'd with thy fires of war!

"And bid around the echoing land
　"The war-horn raise thy vassal powers;
"And, once again, the Bloody Hand §
　"Wave on Dungannon's royal towers!"

---

* The chair of stone on which the chiefs of the O'Neill's were solemnly invested with the power and titles of chief of Tir-owen, and paramount prince of Ulster.

† Hugh O'Nial, illegitimate son of John, formerly chief of Tir-owen, surnamed Ne Gaveloc, or the fettered, from his having been born during the captivity of his mother.

‡ O'Cahan of Cinachta, descended from the famous Cuie-na-gall, or the "Terror of the Stranger," who was celebrated for his exploits against the English.

§ The bloody hand is the crest of the name of O'Neill.

For well that wailing voice he knew,
  And onward hurrying fast.
O'er hills and dales impetuous flew,
  And reach'd his home at last.

Beneath his wearied courser's hoof
  The trembling drawbridge clangs,
And Desmond sees his own good roof,
  But darkness o'er it hangs.

He pass'd beneath the gloomy gate,
  No guiding tapers burn;
No vassals in the court-yard wait,
  To welcome his return.

The hearth is cold in the lonely hall,
  No banquet decks the board;
No page stands ready at the call,
  To 'tend his wearied lord.

But all within is dark and drear,
  No sights or sounds of gladness—
Nought broke the stillness on the ear,
  Save a sudden burst of sadness.

Then slowly swell'd the keener's strain
  With loud lament and weeping,
For round a corse a mournful train
  The sad death-watch were keeping.

Aghast he stood, bereft of power,
  Hope's fairy visions fled;
His fear's confirmed—his beauteous flower—
  His fair-hair'd bride—was dead!

With guarded pace her seasons creep,
 By slow decay expire;
The young above the aged weep,
 The son above the sire:
   Ὠo Cuṁa ! lorn am I !
That death a backward course should hold,
To smite the young, and spare the old.

---

## KATHLEEN'S FETCH.

[The Fetch is supposed to be the exact form and resemblance, as to air, stature, features, and dress, of a certain person, who is soon to depart this world. It is also supposed to appear to the particular friend of the doomed one, and to flit before him without any warning or intimation, but merely the mystery of the appearance at a place and time where and when the real being could not be or appear. It is most frequently thought to be seen when the fated object is about to die a sudden death by unforeseen means, and then it is said to be particularly disturbed and agitated in its motions. Unlike the superstition of the Banshee,* there is no accounting for the coming of this forerunner of death; there is no tracing it to any defined origin; but that it does come, a shadowy phantom of doom and terror, and often comes, is firmly believed by our peasantry, and many curious stories and circumstances are related to confirm the truth of the position.—AUTHOR'S NOTE.]

THE reaper's weary task was done,
And down to repose sunk the autumn sun;
And the crimson clouds, in the rich-hued west,
Were folding like rose leaves round his rest.
My heart was light, and I hummed a tune,
As I hied me home by the harvest moon;
And I bless'd her soft and tender ray,
That rose to lighten my lone pathway.

\* Beaṅrıże.

Then I thought on my Kathleen's winning smile,
(And I felt my heart grow sad the while,)
Of her cheek, like the fading rose-clouds glowing,
Of her hair, like the dying sun-light-flowing;
And her words, like the song of a summer bird,
And her air and step, like the fawn's, when stirred
By the hunter's horn, as it boometh o'er
The woody glens of the steep Sliabh-mor.

The broad Lough Mask* beneath me lay,
Like a sheet of foam in the silver ray;
And its yellow shores were round it rolled,
As a gem enclosed by its fretted gold.
And there, where the old oaks mark the spot,
Arose my Kathleen's sheltered cot;
And I bounded on, for my hopes were high,
Though still at my heart rose the boding sigh.

The silver moon was veiled by a cloud,
And the darkness fell on my soul like a shroud;
And a figure in white was seen afar,
To flit on my path like a twinkling star.
I rushed, I ran,—'twas my Kathleen dear;
But why does she fly? has she aught to fear?
I called, but in vain—like the fleeting beam,
She melted away with the flowing stream.

I came to her father's cottage door,
But the sounds of wailing were on his floor;
And the keener's voice rose loud and wild,
And a mother bewailed her darling child.
My heart grew chill—I could not draw
The latch: I knew 'twas her Fetch I saw!
Yes, Kathleen, fair Kathleen, that sad night died,
The fond pulse of my soul, its hope, its pride

---

* A large and beautiful lake, bounded by the counties of Mayo and
Galway.

## THE DOOM OF THE MIRROR.

### BY B. SIMMONS.

[The superstition that whoever breaks a looking-glass is destined to misfortune, is widely entertained in Ireland. The little story related in these verses is not altogether imaginative.—AUTHOR'S NOTE.]

FAIR Judith Lee—a woful pair,
  Were steed and rider weary,
When, winding down from mountains bare,
  By crag and fastness dreary,
I first beheld her—where the path
  Resigned its sterner traces
In a green depth of woods, like Wrath
  Subdued by Love's embraces.

By the oak-shadowed well she stood,
  Her rounded arms uplifted,
To bind the curls whose golden flood
  Had from its fillets drifted,—
Whilst stooping o'er the fount to fill
  The rustic urn beside her,
Her face to evening's beauty still
  Imparting beauty wider.

She told me of the road I missed—
  Gave me to drink—and even,
At parting, waved the hand she kissed,
  White as a star in heaven;
*But never smiled*—though prompt and warm
  I paid, in duteous phrases,
The tribute that so fair a form
  From minstrel ever raises.

The gladness murmured to her cheek,
  Unfolded not its roses—
That bluest morn will never break
  That in her eye reposes.

Some gentle woe, with dovelike wings,
  Had o'er her cast a shadow,
Soft as the sky of April flings
  Upon a vernal meadow.

In vain, with venial art, to sound
  The springs of that affliction,
I hinted of my *craft*—renowned
  For omen and prediction:
In vain assuming mystic power,
  Her fortune to discover,
I guessed its golden items o'er,
  And closed them with—*a lover*.

It failed for once—that final word—
  A maiden's brow to brighten,
The cloud within her soul unstirred,
  Refused to flash or lighten.
She felt and thanked the artifice,
  Beneath whose faint disguising
I would have prompted hope and peace,
  With accents sympathising.

But no—she said (the while her face
  A summer-wave resembled,
Outsparkling from some leafy place,
  Then back to darkness trembled)—
For her was neither living hope
  Nor loving heart allotted,
Joy had but drawn her horoscope
  For Sorrow's hand to blot it.

Her words made silvery stop—for lo',
  Peals of sweet laughter ringing!
And though that wood's green solitudes
  Glad village-damsels winging!
As thongh that mirth some feeling jarred,
  The maiden, pensive-hearted,
Murmured farewell, and through the dell
  In loneliness departed.

With breeze-tossed locks and gleaming feet,
    And store of slender pitchers,
O'er the dim lawns, like rushing fawns,
    Come the fair Water-fetchers;
And there, while round that well's gray oak
    Cluster'd the sudden glory,
Fair Judith Lee, from guileless lips
    I heard thy simple story.

Of humble lot—the legends wild
    Believed by that condition,
Had mingled with her spirit mild
    Their haunting superstition,
Which grew to grief, when o'er her youth
    The doom descended, spoken
On those who see beneath their touch
    The fatal Mirror broken.

"NEVER IN LIFE TO PROSPER MORE"
    And so, from life sequestred,
With dim forebodings brooding o'er
    The shafted fate that festered
Deep in the white depths of her soul,
    The patient girl awaited
Ill's viewless train—her days to pain
    And duty consecrated.

At times she deemed the coming woe
    Through others' hearts would reach her,
Till every tie that twined her low,
    Upon the lap of Nature
Her once-loved head unwatched, unknown
    Should sink in meek dejection,
Hushed as some Quiet carved in stone
    Above entombed affection.

E'en her young heart's instinctive want
    To be beloved and loving,
Inexorably vigilant,
    She checked with cold reproving.

For still she saw, should tempests frown,
  That treacherous anchor sever,
And Hope's whole priceless freight go down
  A shipwrecked thing for ever.

So pined that gracious form away,
  Her bliss-fraught life untasted;
A breeze-harp whose divinest voice
  On lonely winds is wasted.
And such the tale to me conveyed
  In laughing tones or lowly,
As still that rosy crowd was swayed
  By mirth or melancholy.

I've seen since then the churchyard nook,
  Where Judith Lee lies sleeping;
The wild ash loves it, and a brook
  Through emerald mosses creeping;
For that lost maiden ever there
  A low sweet mass is singing,
While all around, like nuns at prayer,
  Pale water-flowers are springing.

Poor Girl!—I've thought, as there reclined,
  I drank the sunset's glory——
Thy tale to meditative mind
  Is but an allegory;
Once shatter *inborn Truth* divine,
  The soul's transparent mirror,
Where Heaven's reflection loved to shine,
  And what remains but terror?

Terror and Woe;——Faith's holy face
  No more our hearts relieving—
Fades from the past each early grace
  The future brings but grieving;
However fast life's blessings fall
  In lavish sunshine o'er us,
That Broken Glass distorts them all
  Whose fragments glare before us

## THE FAIRY NURSE.

### BY EDWARD WALSH.

[A girl is supposed to be led into the fairy fort of Lisroe, where she sees her little brother, who had died about a week before, laid in a rich cradle, and a young woman singing as she rocks him to sleep. The author has not stated whether there be any meaning in the refrain "Shuheen sho, lulo lo!" which he has introduced after every line. And as there is no Dictionary of the fairy language yet published, I am unable to satisfy myself or the public on that point. I have taken the liberty to omit it, except at the end of each stanza.]

SWEET babe! a golden cradle holds thee,
And soft the snow-white fleece enfolds thee;
In airy bower I'll watch thy sleeping,
Where branchy trees to the breeze are sweeping
   Shuheen sho, lulo lo!

When mothers languish broken-hearted,
When young wives are from husbands parted
Ah! little think the keeners lonely,
They weep some time-worn fairy only.
   Shuheen sho, lulo lo!

Within our magic halls of brightness,
Trips many a foot of snowy whiteness;
Stolen maidens, queens of fairy—
And kings and chiefs a Sluaġ Sía* airy
   Shuheen sho, lulo lo!

Rest thee, babe! I love thee dearly,
And as thy mortal mother nearly;
Ours is the swiftest steed and proudest,
That moves where the tramp of the host is loudest.
   Shuheen sho, lulo lo!

Rest thee, babe! for soon thy slumbers
Shall flee at the magic Coel Sía's† numbers;
In airy bower I'll watch thy sleeping,
Where branchy trees to the breeze are sweeping.
   Shuheen sho, lulo lo!

---

\* Sluagh shee—A Fairy host.    † Koelshie's—Fairy Music

## EARL DESMOND AND THE Beanṅṡide.*

Now cheer thee on, my gallant steed,
  There's a weary way before us—
Across the mountain swiftly speed,
  For the storm is gathering o'er us.

Away, away, the horseman rides;
  His bounding steed's dark form
Seem'd o'er the soft black moss to glide—
  A spirit of the storm!

Now, rolling in the troubled sky,
  The thunder's loudly crashing;
And through the dark clouds, driving by,
  The moon's pale light is flashing.

In sheets of foam the mountain flood
  Comes roaring down the glen;
On the steep bank one moment stood
  The horse and rider then.

One desperate bound the courser gave,
  And plunged into the stream;
And snorting, stemm'd the boiling wave,
  By the lightning's quivering gleam.

The flood is past—the bank is gain'd—
  Away with headlong speed;
A fleeter horse than Desmond rein'd
  Ne'er serv'd at lover's need.

His scatter'd train, in eager haste,
  Far, far behind him ride;
Alone he's crossed the mountain waste,
  To meet his promised bride.

* Banshee.

The clouds across the moon's dim face
  Are fast and faster sailing,
And sounds are heard on the sweeping storm,
  Of wild unearthly wailing.

At first low moanings seem'd to die
  Away, and faintly languish;
Then swell into the piercing cry
  Of deep, heart-bursting anguish.

Beneath an oak, whose branches bare
  Were crashing in the storm,
With wringing hands and streaming hair,
  There sat a female form.

To pass that oak in vain he tried;
  His steed refus'd to stir,
Though furious 'gainst his panting side
  Was struck the bloody spur.

The moon, by driving clouds o'ercast,
  Withheld its fitful gleam;
And louder than the tempest blast
  Was heard the beanrıʒe's scream.

And, when the moon unveiled once more,
  And show'd her paly light,
Then nought was seen save the branches tost
  Of the oak-tree's blasted might.

That shrieking form had vanished
  From out that lonely place;
And, like a dreamy vision, fled,
  Nor left one single trace.

Earl Desmond gaz'd—his bosom swell'd
  With grief and sad foreboding;
Then on his fiery way he held,
  His courser madly goading.

## THE WAKE OF THE ABSENT.

### BY GERALD GRIFFIN

[It is a custom among the peasantry in some parts of Ireland, when any member of a family has been lost at sea (or in any other way which renders the performance of the customary funeral rite impossible), to celebrate the "wake," exactly in the same way, as if the corpse were actually present.]

THE dismal yew, and cypress tall,
  Wave o'er the churchyard lone,
Where rest our friends and fathers all,
  Beneath the funeral stone.
Unvexed in holy ground they sleep,
  Oh early lost! o'er thee
No sorrowing friend shall ever weep,
  Nor stranger bend the knee,
           Mo Cumha! * lorn am I!
Hoarse dashing rolls the salt sea wave,
Over our perished darling's grave—

The winds the sullen deep that tore,
  His death song chanted loud,
The weeds that line the clifted shore
  Were all his burial shroud.
For friendly wail and holy dirge,
  And long lament of love,
Around him roared the angry surge,
  The curlew screamed above,
           Mo Cumha! lorn am I!
My grief would turn to rapture now,
Might I but touch that pallid brow.

The stream-born bubbles soonest burst
  That earliest left the source:
Buds earliest blown are faded first,
  In nature's wonted course:

* Mo Chuma—My grief, or, Woe is me!—T.

## THE BRIDAL WAKE.

### BY GERALD GRIFFIN.

The priest stood at the marriage board,
  The marriage cake was made,
With meat the marriage chest was stored,
  Decked was the marriage bed.
The old man sat beside the fire,
  The mother sat by him,
The white bride was in gay attire,
  But her dark eye was dim.
      Ululah! Ululah!
The night falls quick, the sun is set,
Her love is on the water yet.

I saw a red cloud in the west,
  Against the morning light,
Heaven shield the youth that she loves best
  From evil chance to-night.
The door flings wide! loud moans the gale,
  Wild fear her bosom fills,
It is, it is the Banshee's wail!
  Over the darkened hills.
      Ululah! Ululah!
The day is past! the night is dark!
The waves are mounting round his bark.

The guests sit round the bridal bed,
  And break the bridal cake;
But they sit by the dead man's head,
  And hold his wedding wake.
The bride is praying in her room,
  The place is silent all!
A fearful call! a sudden doom!
  Bridal and funeral.
      Ululah! Ululah!
A youth to Kilfieheras'* ta'en,
That never will return again.

  * The name of a churchyard near Kilken.

## An Caoine.*

### BY CROFTON CROKER.

MAIDENS, sing no more in gladness
  To your merry spinning wheels
Join the keener's voice of sadness—
  Feel for what a mother feels!

See the space within my dwelling—
  'Tis the cold, blank space of death;
'Twas the beanṛiᵹe's† voice came swelling
  Slowly o'er the midnight heath.

Keeners, let your song not falter—
  He was as the hawthorn fair.
Lowly at the Virgin's altar
  Will his mother kneel in prayer.

Prayer is good to calm the spirit,
  When the caoine is sweetly sung:
Death, though mortal flesh inherit,
  Why should age lament the young?

'Twas the beanṛiᵹe's lonely wailing—
  Well I knew the voice of death,
On the night-wind slowly sailing
  O'er the bleak and gloomy heath!

* The keen.      † Banshee.

# HISTORICAL BALLADS.

## THE SAGA OF KING OLAF OF NORWAY, AND HIS DOG.

A.D. 1000.

### BY THOMAS D'ARCY M'GEE.

[Olaf Tryggvesson was King over all Norway from about A.D. 995 to A.D. 1000. His Saga, the sixth in Snorro Sturleson's Heimskringla, is very curious and suggestive. Among other incidents it contains the episode which suggested this Ballad. It may be remarked that the Chronicles of the North-men, of the several nations, throw much reflected light on our own more statistical annals. All through the 9th, 10th, and 11th centuries, that restless race frown along the background of our history, filling us with the same awful interest we feel in watching the advance of one thunder-cloud towards another. They certainly destroyed many native materials for our early history, but in their own accounts of their expeditions into Ireland they have left us much we may use.]

[Of the Early Reign of King Olaf, surnamed Tryggvesson.]

KING OLAF, Harald Haarfager's heir, at last had reached the Throne,
Though his mother bore him in the wilds by a mountain lakelet lone;
Through many a land and danger to his right the King had past,
Uprearing still thro' darkest days, as pines against the blast;

Yet now, when Peace smiled on his Throne, he cast his
    thoughts afar,
And sailed from out the Baltic Sea in search of western
    war—
His Galley was that "Sea-Serpent" renowned in Sagas
    old,
His banner bore two ravens grim—his green mail gleamed
    with gold—
The King's ship and the King himself were glorious to
    behold.

[Of the Sea-King's manner of Life.]

King Olaf was a rover true, his throne was in his
    barque,
The Blue-sea was his royal bath, stars gemm'd his cur-
    tains dark;
The red Sun woke him in the morn, and sailed he e'er
    so far,
The Untired Courier of his way was the ancient Polar
    Star.
It seemed as though the very winds, the clouds, the
    tides, and waves,
Like the sea-side smiths and vikings, were his lieges and
    his slaves.
His Premier was a Pilot old, of bronzed cheek and falcon
    eye,
A Man, albeit who well loved life, yet nothing fear'd
    to die,
Who little knew of Crowns or Courts, and less to crouch
    or lie.

[How King Olaf made a descent on Antrim, and carried off the Herds
thereof.]

Where Antrim's adamantine shore defies the northern
    deep,
O'er Red Bay's broad and buoyant breast, how swift
    the galleys sweep.
The moon is hidden in her height, the night clouds ye
    may see

Flitting like ocean owlets, from the cavern'd shore set
  free.
The full tide slumbers by the cliffs a-weary of its toil,
The goat-herds and their flocks repose upon the upland
  soil :—
The sea-king slowly walks the shore unto his instincts
  true,
While up and down the valley'd landclimbeth his corsair
  crew,
Noiseless as morning mist ascends, or falls the evening
  dew.

[The King is addressed by a Clown, having a marvellous cunning
  dog in his company.]

Now looking to land, and now to sea, the King walked
  on his way,
Until the faint face of the morn gleam'd on the dark-
  some Bay ;
A noble herd of captured kine rank round its ebb-dried
  beach ;
The galleys fast received them in, when lo! with eager
  speech,
A Clown comes headlong from the hills, begging his oxen
  three,
And two white-footed heifers, from the Sov'ran of the
  Sea.
His hurried prayer the King allowed as soon as it he
  heard.
The wolf-hound of the dauntless herd, obedient to his
  word,
Counts out and drives apart his five from the many-
  headed herd.

[King Olaf offereth to purchase the Peasant's dog, who bestows it on
  him with a condition.]

"By Odin, King of Men!" marvelling, the Monarch
  spoke,
"I'll give thee Peasant for thy dog, ten steers of better
  yoke

Than thine own five." The hearty Peasant said:
"King of the Ships, the dog is thine; yet if I must be paid,
Vow, by your raven banner, never again to sack
Our vallies in the hours of night; we dread no day attack."
More wondered the fierce Pagan still to hear a clown so say,
And mused he for a moment, as was his kingly way,
That he should not carry both the man and dog away.

[King Olaf taketh the Vow, and saileth from the shore with the dog.]
The sea-King to the clown made vow, and on his finger placed
An olden ring, the sceptred hand of his great sires had graced,
And round his neck he flung a chain of gold, pure from the mine,
Which, ere another moon, was laid upon St. Colomb's shrine.
Then with his dog he left the shore: his sails swell to the blast;
Poor "Vig" hath howled a mournful cry to the bright shore as they past.
Now brighter beamed the sunrise, and wider spread the tide;
Away, away to the Scottish shore the Danish galleys hied
There, revelling with their kindred, six days they did abide.

[The treason of the Jomsburg Vikings calleth home the King.]
The seventh* news came from Norway, the Vikings had rebelled,
Homeward, homeward, fast as fate, the royal sails are swelled.
Off Halogaland, Jarl Thorer, and Raud the Witch they meet;

* *The Seventh*, meaning the Seventh day.

But a mystic wind bears the evil one unharmed, far
  from the fleet.
Jarl Thorer to the land retreats, the fierce King follows
  on,
Slaying the Traitors' compeer, who fast and far doth
  run.
After him flung King Olaf, his never-missing spear;
But Thorer (he was named Hiort,\* and swifter than
  the deer,)
In the distance took it up, and answered with a jeer.

[Thorer Hiort treacherously killeth the King's Dog.]

The Wolf-Dog then the Monarch loosed, the Traitor
  trembled sore,
Vigorous him on the forest's verge, the King speeds
  from the shore.
Trembled yet more the Caitiff, to think what he should
  do,
He drew his glaive, and with a blow, pierced his captor
  through;
And when the King came to the place, his noble dog lay
  dead,
His red mouth foamy white, and his white breast crimson
  red.
"God's curse upon you, Thorer"—'twas from the heart,
  I ween,
Of the grieved King this ban burst out beside the forest
  green.
——The Traitor vanished into the woods, and never
  again was seen.

[How King Olaf and his Dog were buried nigh unto each other, by the
  Sea.]

Two cairns rise by Drontheim-fiord, with two grey
  stones hard by,
Sculptured with Runic characters, plain to the lore-
  read eye,

\* Literally, a Deer.

And there the King and here his Dog from all their toils
    repose,
And over their cairns the salt sea wind night and day it
    blows;
And close to these they point you the ribs of a galley's
    wreck,
With a forked tongue in the curling crest, and half of a
    scaly neck,
And some late sailing scalds have told that along the
    shore side grey
They have often heard a kindly voice and a huge hound's
    echoing bay,
And some have seen the Traitor to the pine woods run-
    ning away.

---

## Cionn Choppaioh.*

### LAMENTATION OF MAC LIAG FOR KINCORA.—A. D. 1015.

#### TRANSLATED FROM THE IRISH.

#### BY JAMES CLARENCE MANGAN.

[This poem is ascribed to the celebrated poet MAC LIAG, the secretary of the renowned monarch Brian Boru, who, as is well known, fell at the battle of Clontarf in 1014, and the subject of it is a lamentation for the fallen condition of Kincora, the palace of that monarch, consequent on his death.

The decease of MAC LIAG is recorded, in the "Annals of the Four Masters," as having taken place in 1015. A great number of his poems are still in existence, but none of them have obtained a popularity so widely extended as his "Lament."

Of the palace of Kincora, which was situated on the banks of the Shannon, near Killaloe, there are at present no vestiges.]

Oh, where, Kincora! is Brian the Great?
    And where is the beauty that once was thine?
Oh, where are the princes and nobles that sate
    At the feast in thy halls, and drank the red wine
               Where, oh, Kincora?

    * Kincora.

Oh, where, Kincora! are thy valorous lords?
Oh, whither, thou Hospitable! are they gone?
Oh, where are the Dalcassians of the golden swords?*
And where are the warriors Brian led on?
　　　　　　　Where, oh, Kincora?

And where is Morogh, the descendant of kings;
The defeater of a hundred—the daringly brave—
Who set but slight store by jewels and rings;
Who swam down the torrent and laughed at its wave?
　　　　　　　Where, oh, Kincora?

And where is Donogh, King Brian's son?
And where is Conaing, the beautiful chief?
And Kian and Core? Alas! they are gone;
They have left me this night alone with my grief!
　　　　　　　Left me, Kincora!

And where are the chiefs with whom Brian went forth,
The never-vanquished sons of Evin the brave,
The great King of Onaght, renowned for his worth,
And the hosts of Baskinn from the western wave?
　　　　　　　Where, oh, Kincora?

Oh, where is Duvlann of the Swift-footed Steeds?
And where is Kian, who was son of Molloy?
And where is King Lonergan, the fame of whose deeds
In the red battle-field no time can destroy?
　　　　　　　Where, oh, Kincora?

And where is that youth of majestic height,
The faith-keeping Prince of the Scots? Even he,
As wide as his fame was, as great as was his might,
Was tributary, oh Kincora, to thee!
　　　　　　　Thee, oh, Kincora!

---

\* Colġ n-Oṅ (*Colg n-or*) or the Swords *of Gold*, *i. e.* of the Gold-hilted Swords.

They are gone, those heroes of royal birth,
  Who plundered no churches, and broke no trust;
'Tis weary for me to be living on earth
  When they, oh Kincora, lie low in the dust!
        Low, oh, Kincora!

Oh, never again will Princes appear,
  To rival the Dalcassians of the Cleaving Swords:
I can never dream of meeting afar or anear,
  In the east or the west, such heroes and lords!
        Never, Kincora!

Oh, dear are the images my memory calls up
  Of Brian Boru!—how he never would miss
To give me at the banquet the first bright cup!
  Ah! why did he heap on me honour like this?
        Why, oh, Kincora?

I am Mac Liag, and my home is on the Lake:
  Thither often, to that palace whose beauty is fled,
Came Brian, to ask me, and I went for his sake,
  Oh, my grief! that I should live, and Brian be dead!
        Dead, oh, Kincora!

---

## THE DEATH OF KING MAGNUS BAREFOOT.

### A.D. 1102.

#### BY THOMAS D'ARCY M'GEE.

[King Magnus Barefoot became joint king of Norway with Hakon Olatson, in 1093. But Hakon, in chasing a ptarmigan over the Dovrefield, caught an ague, of which he died. After this, Magnus reigned alone for ten years. In this time he made many voyages into the west, conquering all he attacked, whether in the Isles or on the Scottish or English shores. In 1102 he was slain in Ulster by an Irish force, near the sea shore. In Miss Brooke's "Reliques of Irish Poetry" is a translation of an Irish poem on this event, "the author of which" that lady observes, "is said to have belonged to the family of the O'Neills." This poem agrees with Sturleson as to the date of the fight, and its result, but differs in the details. I have followed the latter for the facts of Magnus's previous life, as well as for the immediate cause of his death. It is scarcely necessary to add that at this period the Danes were Christians, in doctrine, if not in practice.]

"On the eve of St. Bartholomew off Ulith's shore we lay,"
(Thus the importuned Scald began his tale of woe,)
"And faintly round our fleet fell the August evening gray,
And sadly the sunset winds did blow.

"I stood beside our Monarch then—deep care was on his brow—
'I hear no horn,' he sighed, 'from the shore:
Why tarry still my errand-men?—'tis time they were here now
And that to some less guarded coast we bore.'

"Into the vernal west our errand-men had gone—
To Muirkeartach, the ally of the King,
(Whose daughter late was wed to Earl Sigurd, his son,)
The dower of the bridegroom to bring.

"'Twas midnight in the firmament, ten thousand stars were there,
And from the darksome sea looked up other ten,
I lay beside our Monarch, he was sleepless, and the care
On his brow had grown gloomier then.

"As the sun awaking bright its beaming lustre shed,
From his couch rose the King slowly up,
'Elldiarn, what!—thou awake! I must landward go,' he said,
'And with you or the saints I shall sup.'

'The while the sun arose, in his galley thro' the fleet
Our noble Magnus went, and the earls all awoke,

And each prepared for land—the late errand men to
 meet,
  Or to free them from the Irish yoke.

" It was a noble army ascending the green hills,
    As ever kingly master led—
 The memory of their marching my mournful bosom
    thrills,
  And my ears catch the echoes of their tread.

" Two hours had passed away, and I wander'd on the
    strand,
    Loud cries from afar smote my ear;
 I climb'd the seaward mountain and look'd upon the land,
    Where, in sooth, I saw a sight of fear.

" As winter-rocks all jagged with the leafless arms of
    pines,
    Stood the Irish host of spears on their path—
 As the winter streams down dash thro' the terrible ra-
    vines,
    So our men sought the shore white with wrath.

" The arrow flights, at intervals, were thicker o'er the
    field
    Than the sea-birds o'er Jura's rocks,
 While the banners in the darkness were lost—shield or
    shield
    Within it clashed in thunderous shocks.

" At last one hoarse *farrah* broke thro' the battle-cloud,
    Like the roar of a billow in a cave;
 And the darkness was uplifted like a plague city's
    shroud,
    And there lifeless lay our Monarch brave.

" And dead beside the king lay Earl Erling's son,
    And Erving and Ulf, the free;
 And loud the Irish cried to see what they had done.
    But they could cry as loud as we.

"Oh! Norway, Norway, wilt thou ever more behold
 A King, like thy last, in worth?
Whose heart feared not the world—whose hands were
     full of gold,
 For the numberless Scalds of the North.

"Ah! well do I remember how he swept the western
     seas
 Like the wind in its wintry mood—
How he reared young Sigurd's throne upon the Orcades,
 And the Isles of the South subdued—

"In his galley o'er Cantire, how we bore him from the
     main—
 How Mona in a week he won;
By him, how Chester's Earl in Anglesea was slain—
 Oh! Norway, that his course is run!"

---

## THE BATTLE OF Cnoc-Cuaö.\*

### A.D. 1189.

#### BY THE AUTHOR OF "THE MONKS OF KILCREA."

[About this time (1189) the Anglo-Norman power in Ireland received a severe check by the death of Sir Armoricus Tristram, brother-in-law, and, after the chivalrous fashion of the day, sworn comrade of Sir John De Courcey Having gone with a strong force to Connaught on an expedition, he was attacked with a far superior army by Cathal O'Connor,† surnamed "The Red Handed," and slain, with all his followers.]

Close hemm'd by foes, in Ulster hills, within his castle
     pent,
For aid unto the west countrie Sir John De Courcey
     sent;

---

\* Knocktuadh, "The Hill of Axes," lies within a few miles of Galway.
† For an exquisite ballad on "Cathal O'Connor" see p. 114.

And, for the sake of knightly vow, and friendship old
    and tried,
He prayed that Sir Armor Tristram would to his rescue
    ride.

Then grieved full sore that noble knight, when he those
    tidings heard,
And deep a vow he made, with full many a holy
    word—
That, aid him Heaven and good St. Lawrence, full
    vengence should await
The knaves who did De Courcey wrong, and brought
    him to this strait.

And a goodly sight it was, o'er Clare-Galway's glassy
    plain,
To see the bold Sir Tristram pass, with all his gallant
    train:
For thirty knights came with him there, all kinsmen
    of his blood,
And seven score spears and ten, right valiant men
    and good.

And clasping close, with sturdy arms, each horseman
    by the waist,
Behind each firm-fixed saddle there, a footman light was
    placed;
And fast they spurred in sweeping trot, as if in utmost
    need,
Their harness ringing loudly round, and foam upon
    each steed.

They cross the stream—they reach the wood—the bend-
    ing boughs give way,
And fling upon their waving plumes light showers of
    sparkling spray;
But when they pass that leafy copse, and topp'd the
    hillock's crest,
Then jumped each footman down—each horseman laid
    his lance in rest.

For far and wide as eye could reach, a mighty host was
  seen
Of Irish kernes and gallowglass, with hobbelers between,
And proudly waving in the front fierce Cathal's standard
  flies,
With many more of Cannaught's chiefs, and Desmond's
  tribes likewise.

Then to a knight Sir Tristram spake, with fearless eye
  and brow,
"Sir Hugolin, advance my flag, and do this errand
  now:
Go, seek the leader of yon host, and greet him fair
  from me,
And ask, why thus, with armed men, he blocks my
  passage free?"

Then stout Sir Hugolin prick'd forth, upon his gallant
  gray,
The banner in his good right hand, and thus aloud did
  say:—
"Ho! Irish chiefs! Sir Armor Tristram greets ye fair,
  by me,
And bids me ask, why thus in arms ye block his passage free?"

Then stept fierce Cathal to the front, his chieftains
  standing nigh:
"Proud stranger, take our answer back, and this our
  reason why:—
Our wolves are gaunt for lack of food—our eagles
  pine away,
And to glut them with your flesh, lo! we stop you
  here this day!"

"Now, gramercy for the thought!" calm Sir Hugolin
  replied,
And with a steadfast look and mien that wrathful chief
  he eyed:—

"Yet, should your wild birds covet not the dainty
  fare you name,
Then, by the rood, our Norman swords shall carve them
  better game!"

Then turned his horse, and back he rode unto the
  little band
That, halted on the hill, in firm and martial order stand;
When told his tale, then divers knights began to counsel take,
How best they could their peril shun, and safe deliverance make.

"Against such odds, all human might is valueless!"
  they cried;
"And better 'twere at once to turn, and thro' the
  thicket ride."
When, high o'er all, Sir Tristram spake, in accents bold
  and free:—
"Let all depart who fear to fight this battle out with
  me;

"For never yet shall mortal say, I left him in his need,
Or brought him into danger's grasp—then trusted to
  my steed!
And, come what will, whate'er betide, let all depart who
  may,
I'll share my comrades' lot, and with them stand or fall
  this day!"

Then drooped with burning shame full many a knightly
  crest,
And nobler feelings answering swell'd throughout each
  throbbing breast;
And stout Sir Hugolin spoke first:—"Whate'er our
  lot may be,
Come weal, come woe, 'fore Heaven, we'll stand or fall
  this day with thee!"

Then from his horse Sir Tristram lit, and drew his
  shining blade

And gazing on the noble beast, right mournfully he said :—
"Thro' many a bloody field thou hast borne me safe and well,
And never knight had truer friend than thou, fleet Roancelle!

"When wounded sore, and left for dead, on far Knockgara's plain,
No friendly aid or vassal near—yet, thou did'st still remain !
Close to thy master there thou madest thy rough and fearful bed,
And on thy side, that night, my steed, I laid my aching head !

"Yet now, my gallant horse, we part! thy proud career is o'er,
And never shalt thou bound beneath an armed rider more."
He spoke, and kist the blade—then pierced his charger's glossy side,
And madly plunging in the air, the noble courser died !

Then every horseman in his band, dismounting, did the same,
And in that company no steed alive was left, but twain;
On one there rode De Courcey's squire, who came from Ulster wild ;
Upon the other young Oswald sate, Sir Tristram's only child.

The father kist his son, then spake, while tears his eyelids fill :
"Good Hamo, take my boy, and spur with him to yonder hill ;
Go, watch from thence, till all is o'er; then, northward haste in flight,
And say, that Tristram in his harness died, like a worthy knight."

Now pealed along the foeman's ranks a shrill and wild
   halloo!
While boldly back defiance loud the Norman bugles
   blew;
And bounding up the hill, like hounds, at hunted
   quarry set,
The Irish kernes came fiercely on, and fiercely were
   they met.

Then rose the roar of battle loud —the shout—the cheer
   —the cry !
The clank of ringing steel, the gasping groans of those
   who die ;
Yet onward still the Norman band, right fearless cut
   their way,
As move the mowers o'er the sward upon a summer's
   day.

For round them there, like shorn grass, the foe in hundreds bleed ;
Yet, fast as e'er they fall, each side, do hundreds more
   succeed
With naked breasts, undaunted meet the spears of steel-
   clad men,
And sturdily, with axe and skein, repay their blows
   again.

Now, crushed with odds, their phalanx broke, each Norman fights alone,
And few are left throughout the field, and they are fee-
   ble grown ;
But, high o'er all, Sir Tristram's voice is like a trumpet
   heard,
And still, where'er he strikes, the foemen sink beneath
   his sword.

But once he raised his beaver up—alas ! it was to try
If Hamo and his boy yet tarried on the mountain
   nigh;

When sharp an arrow from the foe, pierc'd right thro'
　　his brain,
And sank the gallant knight a corpse upon the bloody
　　plain.

Then failed the fight, for gathering round his lifeless
　　body there,
The remnant of his gallant band fought fiercely in de-
　　spair;
And one by one they wounded fell—yet with their latest
　　breath,
Their Norman war-cry shouted bold—then sank in silent
　　death.

And thus Sir Tristram died; than whom no mortal
　　knight could be
More brave in list or battle-field,—in banquet-hall more
　　free;
The flower of noble courtesy—of Norman peers the
　　pride;
Oh, not in Christendom's wide realms can be his loss
　　supplied.

Sad tidings these to tell, in far Downpatrick's lofty
　　towers,
And sadder news to bear to lone Ivora's silent bowers;
Yet shout ye not, ye Irish kernes—good cause have ye
　　to rue;
For a bloody fight and stern was the battle of Cnoc
　　Cuad.

## A VISION OF Conact* IN THE THIRTEENTH CENTURY.

### BY JAMES CLARENCE MANGAN.

"Et moi, j'ai ete aussi en Arcadie."—And I, I, too, have been a dreamer.—*Inscription on a Painting by Poussin.*

I walked entranced
 Through a land of morn;
The sun, with wondrous excess of light,
 Shone down and glanced
 Over seas of corn,
And lustrous gardens aleft and right.
 Even in the clime
 Of resplendent Spain
Beams no such sun upon such a land:
 But it was the time,
 'Twas in the reign,
Of Cáhal Mór of the Wine-red Hand.†

Anon stood nigh
 By my side a man
Of princely aspect and port sublime.
 Him queried I,
 "O, my Lord and Khan,‡
What clime is this, and what golden time?"
 When he—"The clime
 Is a clime to praise,
The clime is Erin's, the green and bland;
 And it is the time,
 These be the days,
Of Cáhal Mór of the Wine-red Hand!"

\* Connaught.

† The Irish and Oriental poets both agree in attributing favourable or unfavourable weather and abundant or deficient harvests to the good or bad qualities of the reigning monarch. What the character of Cahal was will be seen below.

‡ Identical with the Irish *Ceann*, Head, or Chief; but I the rather gave him the Oriental title, as really fancying myself in one of the regions of Araby the Blest.

Then I saw thrones,
    And circling fires,
And a dome rose near me, as by a spell
    Whence flowed the tones
      Of silver lyres
And many voices in wreathed swell;
    And their thrilling chime
      Fell on mine ears
As the heavenly hymn of an angel-band—
    "It is now the time,
      These be the years,
Of Cáhal Mór of the Wine-red Hand!"


I sought the hall,
    And, behold!—a change
From light to darkness, from joy to woe
    Kings, nobles, all,
      Looked aghast and strange;
The minstrel-group sate in dumbest show;
    Had some great crime
      Wrought this dread amaze,
This terror? None seemed to understand!
    'Twas then the time,
      We were in the days,
Of Cáhal Mór of the Wine-red Hand.


I again walked forth;
    But lo! the sky
Showed fleckt with blood, and an alien sun
    Glared from the north,
      And there stood on high,
Amid his shorn beams, A SKELETON!*

---

* "It was but natural that these portentous appearances should thus be exhibited on this occasion, for they were the heralds of a very great calamity that befe the Connacians in this year—namely, the death of Cathal of the Red Hand, son of Torlogh Mor of the Wine, and king of Connaught, a prince of most amiable qualities, and into whose heart GOD had infused more piety and goodness than into the hearts of any of his cotemporaries."—*Annals of the Four Masters, A.D. 1224.*

It was by the stream
Of the castled Maine,
One autumn eve, in the Teuton's land,
That I dreamed this dream
Of the time and reign
Of Cáhal Mór of the Wine-red Hand!

## BATTLE OF CREDRAN.

A.D. 1257.

### BY EDWARD WALSH.

[A brilliant battle was fought by Geoffrey O'Donnell, Lord of Tirconnell, against the Lord Justice of Ireland, Maurice Fitzgerald, and the English of Connaught, at Credran Cille, Roseede, in the territory of Carburry, north of Sligo, in defence of his principality. A fierce and terrible conflict took place, in which bodies were hacked, heroes disabled, and the strength of both sides exhausted. The men of Tirconnell maintained their ground, and completely overthrew the English forces in the engagement, and defeated them with great slaughter; but Geoffrey himself was severely wounded, having encountered in the fight Maurice Fitzgerald, in single combat, in which they mortally wounded each other.—*Annals of the Four Masters, translated by Owen Connellan, Esq.*]

From the glens of his fathers O'Donnell comes forth,
With all Cinel-Conaill,* fierce septs of the North—
O'Boyle and O'Daly, O'Dugan, and they
That own, by the wild waves, O'Doherty's sway.

Clan Connor, brave sons of the diadem'd Niall,
Has pour'd the tall clansmen from mountain and vale—
M'Sweeny's sharp axes, to battle oft bore,
Flash bright in the sun-light by high Dunamore.

* *Cinel-Conaill*—The descendants of Conall-Gulban, the son of Nial of the Nine Hostages, Monarch of Ireland in the fourth century. The principality was named Tir-Chonaile, or Tyrconnell, which included the county Donegal, and its chiefs were the O'Donnells.

Through Inis-Mac-Durin,* through Derry's dark
   brakes,
Glentocher of tempests, Sleibh-sneacht of the lakes,
Bundoran of dark spells, Loch-Suileach's rich glen,
The red deer rush wild at the war-shout of men!

O! why through Tir-Chonaill, from Cuil-dubh's dark
   steep,
To Samer's † green border the fierce masses sweep,
Living torrents o'er-leaping their own river shore,
In the red sea of battle to mingle their roar?

Stretch thy vision far southward, and seek for reply
Where blaze of the hamlets glares red on the sky—
Where the shrieks of the hopeless rise high to their
   God,
Where the foot of the Sassanach spoiler has trod!

Sweeping on like a tempest, the Gall-Oglach ‡ stern
Contends for the van with the swift-footed kern—
There's blood for that burning, and joy for that wail—
The avenger is hot on the spoiler's red trail!

The Saxon hath gather'd on Credran's far heights,
His groves of long lances, the flower of his knights—
His awful cross-bowmen, whose long iron hail
Finds, through Cota § and Sciath, the bare heart of the
   Gael!

The long lance is brittle—the mailèd ranks reel
Where the Gall-Oglach's axe hews the harness of steel;
And truer to its aim in the breast of a foeman,
Is the pike of a kern than the shaft of a bowman.

* Districts in Donegal.
† *Samer*—The ancient name of Loch Earne.
‡ *Gall-Oglach, or Gallowglass*—The heavy-armed foot soldier. *Kern,
or Ceithernach*—The light-armed soldier.
§ *Cota*—The saffron-dyed shirt of the kern, consisting of many yards
of yellow linen thickly plaited. *Sciath*—The wicker shield, as its name
imports.

One prayer to St. Columb\*—the battle-steel clashes—
The tide of fierce conflict tumultuously dashes;
Surging onward, high-heaving its billow of blood,
While war-shout and death-groan swell high o'er the flood!

As meets the wild billows the deep-centr'd rock,
Met glorious Clan Chonaill the fierce Saxon's shock;
As the wrath of the clouds flash'd the axe of Clan-Chonaill,
Till the Saxon lay strewn 'neath the might of O'Donnell!

One warrior alone holds the wide bloody field,
With barbed black charger and long lance and shield—
Grim, savage, and gory he meets their advance,
His broad shield up-lifting and crouching his lance.

Then forth to the van of that fierce rushing throng
Rode a chieftain of tall spear and battle-axe strong,
His bracca,† and geochal, and cochal's red fold,
And war-horse's housings, were radiant in gold!

Say who is this chief spurring forth to the fray,
The wave of whose spear holds yon armed array?
And he who stands scorning the thousands that sweep,
An army of wolves over shepherdless sheep?

---

\* *St. Colum*, or *Colum-Cille, the dove of the Church*— The patron saint of Tyrconnell, descended from Conall Gulban.

† *Bracca*—So called, from being striped with various colours, was the tight-fitting Iruis. It covered the ancles, legs, and thighs, rising as high as the loins, and fitted so tight to the limbs as to discover every muscle and motion of the parts which it covered.—*Walker on Dress of the Irish*.

*Geochal*—The jacket made of gilded leather, and which was sometimes embroidered with silk —*Ibid*.

*Cochal*—A sort of cloak with a large hanging collar of different colours. This garment reached to the middle of the thigh, and was fringed with a border like shagged hair, and being brought over the shoulders was fastened on the breast by a clasp, buckle, or brooche of silver or gold. In battle, they wrapped the Cochal several times round the left arm as a shield.—*Ibid*.

The shield of his nation, brave Geoffrey O'Donnell
(Clar-Fodhla's firm prop is the proud race of Conaill).\*
And Maurice Fitzgerald, the scorner of danger,
The scourge of the Gael, and the strength of the stranger.

The launch'd spear hath torn through target and mail—
The couch'd lance hath borne to his crupper the Gael—
The steeds driven backwards all helplessly reel;
But the lance that lies broken hath blood on its steel!

And now fierce O'Donnell, thy battle-axe wield—
The broad-sword is shiver'd, and cloven the shield,
The keen steel sweeps grinding through proud crest and
    crown—
Clar-Fodlah hath triumph'd—the Saxon is down!

## THE BATTLE OF ARDNOCHER.

### A.D. 1328.

**BY THE AUTHOR OF "THE MONKS OF KILCREA."**

[A.D. 1328, MacGeoghegan gave a great overthrow to the English, in which three thousand five hundred of them, together with the D'Altons, were slain.—*Annals of the Four Masters.*

This battle, in which the English forces met such tremendous defeat, was fought near Mullingar, on the day before the feast of St. Laurence—namely, the 9th August. The Irish clans were commanded by William MacGeoghegan, Lord of Kenil Feacha, in Westmeath, comprising the present baronies of Moycashel and Rathconrath. The English forces were commanded by Lord Thomas Butler, the Petits, Tuites, Nangles. Delemers, &c. The battle took place at the Hill of Ardnocher.—*Ibid*, p. 116.]

On the eve of St. Laurence, at the cross of Glenfad,
Both of chieftains and bonaghts what a muster we had,

---

\* This is the translation of the first line of a poem of two hundred and forty-eight verses, written by Firgal og Mac-an-Bhaird on Dominick O'Donnell, in the year 1655. The original line is—
    "Gaibhle Fodhla fuil Chonaill."
—*See O'Reilly's Account of Irish Writers.*

Thick as bees, round the heather, on the side of Slieve
Bloom,
To the trysting they gather by the light of the moon.

For The Butler from Ormond with a hosting he came,
And harried Moyeashel with havoc and flame,
Not a hoof or a hayrick, nor corn blade to feed on,
Had he left in the wide land, right up to Dunbreedon.

Then gathered MacGeoghegan, the high prince of Donore,
With O'Connor from Croghan, and O'Dempsys 30
león ;*
And, my soul, how we shouted, as dash'd in with their
men,
Bold MacCoghlan from Clara, O'Mulloy from the glen

And not long did we loiter where the four ⲧⲟⲥⲁⲣⲥ† met,
But his saddle each tightened, and his spurs closer set,
By the skylight that flashes all their red burnings back,
And by black gore and ashes fast the reivers we track.

'Till we came to Ardnocher, and its steep slope we gain,
And stretch'd there, beneath us, saw their host in the
plain ;
And high shouted our leader ('twas the brave William
Roe)—
"By the red hand of Nial, 'tis the Sassanach foe!"

"Now, low level your spears, grasp each battle-axe firm,
And for God and our Ladye strike ye downright and
stern ;
For our homes and our altars charge ye steadfast and
true,
And our watchword be vengeance, and Láṁ Ðeaṛɼ
Abu !‡"

* Galore (in abundance). † Toghers (roads).
‡ Lamh Dearg Aboo (the red hand for ever).

Oh, then down like a torrent with a *farrah* we swept,
And full stout was the Saxon who his saddle-tree kept;
For we dash'd thro' their horsemen till they reel'd from
   the stroke,
And their spears, like dry twigs, with our axes we broke.

With our plunder we found them, our fleet garrons and
   kine,
And each chalice and cruet they had snatch'd from God's
   shrine.
But a red debt we paid them, the Sassanach raiders,
As we scatter'd their spearmen, slew chieftains and
   leaders.

In the Pale there is weeping and watchings in vain.
De Lacy and D'Alton, can ye reckon your slain?
Where's your chieftain, fierce Nangle? Has De Netter-
   ville fled?
Ask the Molingar eagles, whom their carcasses fed.

Ho! ye riders from Ormond, will ye brag in your hall,
How your lord was struck down with his mail'd knights
   and all?
Swim at midnight the Shannon, beard the wolf in his
   den,
Ere you ride to Moycashel on a foray again!

## Ɡɼáınne Ṁaol* AND ELIZABETH.

### A.D. 1575.

#### BY THE AUTHOR OF "THE MONKS OF KILCREA."†

[The following account of Ɡɼáınne Ṁaol is taken from Owen Connelan's Translation of the "Annals of the Four Masters," note ɔ. 547; it is compiled from Articles in the *Anthologia Hibernica*, Lodge's *Peerage of Ireland*, and other authorities.

Grace O'Malley, called in Irish Ɡɼáınne Ṁaol, commonly pronounced *Granu Wail*, is celebrated in Irish History. She was first married to O'Flaherty, Chief of West Connaught; and, secondly, to Sir Richard Burke, by whom she had a son Theobald, who was a commander of note on the side of the English, in Connaught, in the reign of Elizabeth; he was called Sir Theobald Burke, and was created Viscount of Mayo by Charles I. Her father, Owen O'Malloy, was a noted chief, and had a small fleet with which he made many expeditions, partly for commercial purposes, but chiefly in piracy. Grace, in her youth, frequently accompanied her father on these expeditions, and after his death, her brother being a minor, she took upon herself the command of her galleys, and made with her crews many bold expeditions; her chief rendezvous was at Clare Island, off the coast of Mayo, where she kept her large vessels moored, and had a fortress; but she had her small craft at Carrigahooly ‡ Castle (in the bay of Newport, county Mayo), which was her chief residence and stronghold; and there was a hole to be seen in the ruined walls through which a cable was run from one of her ships, for the purpose of communicating an alarm to her apartment on any sudden danger. It is said that her piracies became so frequent that she was proclaimed, and £500 offered as a reward for her apprehension, and troops were sent from Galway to take the Castle of Carrigahooly, but after a siege of more than a fortnight, they were forced to retire, being defeated by the valour of Grace and her men. These exploits were performed by her before and after her marriage with O'Flaherty, but after his death, and her marriage with Sir Richard Burke, she became reconciled to the government, and, with her followers, assisted the English forces in Connaught, and for her services it is said that Queen Elizabeth wrote her a letter of invitation to the court, in consequence of which Grace, with some of her galleys, set sail for London, about the year 1575, and she was re-

---

\* Grainne Maol—pronounced *Granu Wail.*
† See "Ballad Poetry of Ireland," p. 227.
‡ Caɼɼaıcc-a-Uıle. (Carrick-a-Uile—the **Rock in the Elbow.**)

ceived at court with great honours by the Queen, who offered to create her a Countess, which honour Grace declined, answering that both of them being Princesses, they were equal in rank, and they could therefore confer no honours on each other: but Grace said that her Majesty might confer any title she pleased on her young son, a child which was born on ship-board during her voyage to England; and it is said that the Queen knighted the child, who was called by the Irish Tiobold-na-Lung,\* signifying Theobald of the Ships, from the circumstance of his being born on ship-board, and this Sir Theobald Burke was created Viscount of Mayo by Charles I.

The well-known circumstance of her carrying off the young heir of St. Laurence from Howth, as a punishment for his father's want of hospitality in having the Castle gates closed during dinner time, occurred on her return from England.

Grace endowed a monastery on Clare Island, off the coast of Mayo, where she was buried, and it is said some remains of her monument are still to be seen there.

Grace O'Malley has been long famous as an Irish heroine in the traditions of the people, and her name is still remembered in song; in various poetical compositions, both in English and Irish, her name is celebrated; and in these songs Ireland is generally personified under the designation of Granu Wail. One of these, which was very popular, was composed by the celebrated Jacobite Munster Bard, Shane Clarach Mac Donnell.]

There stands a tower by the Atlantic side—
   A gray old tower, by storms and sea-waves beat—
Perch'd on a cliff beneath it, yawneth wide
   A lofty cavern—of yore, a fit retreat
   For pirates' galleys; altho' now, you'll meet
Nought but the seal and wild gull; from that cave
   A hundred steps doth upwards lead your feet
Unto a lonely chamber!—bold and brave
Is he who climbs that stair, all slippery from the wave

I sat there on an evening. In the west,
   Amid the waters, sank the setting sun;
While clouds, like parting friends, about him prest,
   Clad in their fleecy garbs, of gold and dun;
   And silence was around me—save the hum
Of the lone wild bee, or the curlew's cry.
   And lo! upon me did a vision come,
Of her who built that tower, in days gone by
And, in that dream, behold! I saw a building

\* Tioboid-na-Lung.

A stately hall—lofty and carved the roof—
   Was deck'd with silken banners fair to see.
The hangings velvet, from Genoa's woof,
   And wrought with Tudor roses curiously;
   At its far end did stand a canopy,
Shading a chair of state, on which was seen
   A ladye fair, whose look of majesty,
Amid a throng, 'yclad in costly sheen—
Nobles and gallant knights proclaimed her England's
   Queen!

The sage Elizabeth! and by her side
   Were group'd her counsellors, with calm grave air,
Burleigh and Walsingham, with others, tried
   In wisdom and in war, and sparkling there,
   Like Summer butterflies, were damsels fair,
Beautiful and young: behind a trusty band
   Of stalwart yeomanry, with watchful care,
The portal guard, while nigher to it stand
Usher and page, ready to ope with willing hand.

A Tucket sounds, and lo! there enters now
   A stranger group, in saffron tunics drest:
A female at their head, whose step and brow
   Herald her rank, and calm and self possest
   Onward she comes, alone, through England's best,
With careless look and bearing free, yet high.
   Tho' gentle dames their titterings scarce represt,
Noting her garments as she past them by;
None laughed again, who met that stern and flashing
   eye.

Restless and dark, its sharp and rapid look
   Shew'd a fierce spirit, prone a wrong to feel,
And quicker to revenge it. As a Book,
   That sun-burnt brow did fearless thoughts reveal:
   And in her girdle was a skeyne of steel;
Her crimson mantle, a gold brooch did bind;
   Her flowing garments reached unto her heel;

Her hair—part fell in tresses unconfined,
And part, a silver bodkin did fasten up behind.*

'Twas not her garb that caught the gazers' eye—
  Tho' strange, 'twas rich, and after its fashion, good—
But the wild grandeur of her mien—erect and high.
  Before the English Queen she dauntless stood,
  And none her bearing there could scorn as rude;
She seemed well used to power—as one that hath
  Dominion over man of savage mood,
And dared the tempest in its midnight wrath,
And thro' opposing billows cleft her fearless path.

And courteous greeting Elizabeth then pays,
  And bids her welcome to her English land
And humble hall. Each look with curious gaze
  Upon the other's face, and felt they stand
Before a spirit like their own. Her hand
The stranger raised—and pointing where all pale,
  Thro' the high casement, came the sunlight bland,
Gilding the scene and group with rich avail;
Thus, to the English Sov'reign, spoke proud Grainne
    Waol:

"Queen of the Saxons! from the distant west
  I come; from Achill steep and Island Clare,
Where the wild eagle builds, 'mid clouds, his nest,
  And ocean flings its billows in the air.
  I come to greet you in your dwelling fair.
Led by your fame—lone sitting in my cave,
  In sea-beat Doona---it hath reached me there,
Theme of the minstrel's song; and then I gave
My galley to the wind, and crossed the dark green
    wave.

---

*. A yellow bodice and petticoat. Her hair gathered to the crown and fastened with a bodkin, with a crimson mantle thrown over her shoulders, constituted the court dress of the Irish heroine.—*Wright's Scenes in Ireland.*

"Health to thee, ladye!---let your answer be,
  Health to our Irish land; for evil men
Do vex her sorely, and have bucklar'd thee
  Abettor of their deeds; a lying train,
  That cheat their mistress for the love of gain,
And wrong their trust---aught else I little reck,
  Alike to me, the mountain and the glen---
The castle's rampart or the galley's deck;
But thou my country spare---your foot is on her neck'

Thus brief and bold, outspake that ladye stern,
  And all stood silent thro' that crowded hall;
While proudly glared each wild and savage kern
  Attendant on their mistress. Then courtly all
  Elizabeth replies, and soothing fall
Her words, and pleasing to the Irish ear---
  Fair promises---that she would soon recal
Her evil servants. Were these words sincere?---
That promise kept? Let Erin answer with a tear.

And such my dream, by distant Erris' side,
  Where Clare's tall cliffs opposed the dashing sea.
Lone Isle of storms! tho' years have multiplied
  Since first in boyhood's prime I gazed on thee,
  And thus amid thy towers held reverie;
Yet thou art fresh before me!---even here
  Where glides, 'mid verdant banks, the gentle Lee
I seem to see thee, 'gainst the horizon clear,
And oft thy many-billowed surge I fancy near.

## THE DEATH OF SCHOMBERG.

### A.D. 1690.

### BY DIGBY PILOT STARKEY.

[" Frederick Schonberg, or Schomberg, first developed his warlike talents under the command of Henry and William II. of Orange; afterwards obtained several victories over the Spaniards; reinstated on the throne the house of Braganza; defeated in England the last hopes of the Stuarts; and finally died at the advanced age of eighty-two, at the battle of the Boyne, in 1690."]

'TWAS on the day when Kings did fight beside the Boyne's dark water,
And thunder roar'd from every height, and earth was red with slaughter,—
That morn an aged chieftain stood apart from mustering bands,
And, from a height that crown'd the flood, surveyed broad Erin's lands.

His hand upon his sword-hilt leant, his war-horse stood beside,
And anxiously his eyes were bent across the rolling tide:
He thought of what a changeful fate had borne him from the land
Where frown'd his father's castle-gate,* high o'er the Rhenish strand,

And plac'd before his opening view a realm where strangers bled,
Where he, a leader, scarcely knew the tongue of those he led!

---

* Schonberg, or "the mount of beauty," is one of the most magnificent of the many now ruinous castles that overhang the Rhine.— It had been the residence of the chiefs of a noble family of that name, which existed as far back as the time of Charlemagne, and of which the Duke of Schomberg was a member.

He looked upon his chequered life, from boyhood's earliest time,
Through scenes of tumult and of strife, endur'd in every clime,

To where the snows of eighty years usurped the raven's stand,
And still the din was in his ears, the broadsword in his hand!
He turn'd him to futurity, beyond the battle plain,
But then a shadow from on high hung o'er the heaps of slain;—

And through the darkness of the cloud, the chief's prophetic glance
Beheld, with winding-sheet and shroud, his fatal hour advance:
He quail'd not, as he felt him near th' inevitable stroke,
But, dashing off one rising tear, 'twas thus the old man spoke:

" God of my fathers! death is nigh, my soul is not deceived—
My hour is come, and I would die the conqueror I have liv'd;
For thee, for freedom, have I stood—for both I fall to-day;
Give me but victory for my blood, the price I gladly pay!

" Forbid the future to restore a Stuart's despot-gloom,
Or that, by freemen dreaded more, the tyranny of Rome!
From either curse, let Erin freed, as prosperous ages run,
Acknowledge what a glorious deed upon this day was done!"

He said: fate granted *half* his prayer. His steed he
    straight bestrode,
And fell, as on the routed rear of James's host he rode.
He sleeps in a cathedral's gloom,* amongst the mighty
    dead,
And frequent, o'er his hallow'd tomb, redeedful pilgrims
    tread.
The other half, though fate deny, we'll strive for, one
    and all;
And William's—Schomberg's spirits nigh, we'll gain—er,
    fighting, fall!

1833.

---

## THE BATTLE OF THE BOYNE.

### A.D. 1690.

### BY COLONEL BLACKER.

It was upon a summer's morn, unclouded rose the sun,
And lightly o'er the waving corn their way the breezes
    won;
Sparkling beneath that orient beam, 'mid banks of ver-
    dure gay,
Its eastward course a silver stream held smilingly away.

A kingly host upon its side a monarch camp'd around,
Its southern upland far and wide their white pavilions
    crowned;
Not long that sky unclouded show'd, nor long beneath
    the ray
That gentle stream in silver flowed, to meet the new-
    born day.

* St. Patrick's, Dublin.

Through yonder fairy-haunted glen, from out that dark
    ravine,*
Is heard the tread of marching men, the gleam of arms
    is seen;
And plashing forth in bright array along yon verdant
    banks,
All eager for the coming fray, are rang'd the martial
    ranks.

Peals the loud gun—its thunders boom the echoing vales
    along,
While curtain'd in its sulph'rous gloom moves on the
    gallant throng;
And foot and horse in mingled mass, regardless all of
    life,
With furious ardour onward pass to join the deadly
    strife.

Nor strange that with such ardent flame each glowing
    heart beats high,
Their battle word was William's name, and "Death or
    Liberty!"
Then, Oldbridge, then thy peaceful bowers with sounds
    unwonted rang,
And Tredagh, 'mid thy distant towers, was heard the
    mighty clang;

The silver stream is crimson'd wide, and clogg'd with
    many a corse,
As floating down its gentle tide come mingled man and
    horse.
Now fiercer grows the battle's rage, the guarded stream
    is cross'd,
And furious, hand to hand engage each bold contending
    host;

He falls—the veteran hero falls,† renowned along the
    Rhine—

* King William's Glen, near Townley Hall.
† Duke Schomberg.

And he, whose name, while Derry's walls endure, shall
  brightly shine.\*
Oh! would to heav'n that churchman bold, his arms
  with triumph blest,
The soldier spirit had controll'd that fir'd his pious
  breast.

And he, the chief of yonder brave and persecuted band,†
Who foremost rush'd amid the wave, and gain'd the
  hostile strand;—
He bleeds, brave Caillemote—he bleeds—'tis clos'd, his
  bright career,
Yet still that band to glorious deeds his dying accents
  cheer.

And now that well contested strand successive columns
  gain,
While backward James's yielding band are borne across
  the plain.
In vain the sword green Erin draws, and life away doth
  fling—
Oh! worthy of a better cause and of a bolder king.

In vain thy bearing bold is shown upon that blood-
  stain'd ground;
Thy tow'ring hopes are overthrown, thy choicest fall
  around.
Nor, sham'd, abandon thou the fray, nor blush, though
  conquer'd there,
A power against thee fights to-day no mortal arm may
  dare.

Nay, look not to that distant height in hope of coming
  aid—
The dastard thence has ta'en his flight, and left his men
  betray'd.

\* Walker, the gallant defender of Derry.
† Caillemote, who commanded a regiment of

Hurrah! hurrah! the victor shout is heard on high
 Donore;
Down Platten's vale, in hurried rout, thy shatter'd
 masses pour.

But many a gallant spirit there retreats across the
 plain.
Who, change but kings, would gladly dare that battle
 field again.*
Enough! enough! the victor cries; your fierce pursuit
 forbear,
Let grateful prayer to heaven arise, and vanquished
 freemen spare.

Hurrah! hurrah! for liberty, for her the sword we
 drew,
And dar'd the battle, while on high our Orange banners
 flew;
Woe worth the hour—woe worth the state, when men
 shall cease to join
With grateful hearts to celebrate the glories of the
 Boyne!

\* This alludes to the expression attributed to Sarsfield—" Only
change kings, and we will fight the battle over again."

# DESCRIPTIVE BALLADS.

## LAMENT OVER THE RUINS OF THE ABBEY OF

## Teach Molaga.*

### TRANSLATED FROM THE IRISH.

#### BY SAMUEL FERGUSON, M.R.I.A.

Lone and weary as I wander'd by the bleak shore of the sea,
Meditating and reflecting on the world's hard destiny,
Forth the moon and stars 'gan glimmer, in the quiet tide beneath,
For on slumbering spring and blossom breathed not out of heaven a breath.

On I went in sad dejection, careless where my footsteps bore,
Till a ruined church before me opened wide its ancient door,—
Till I stood before the portals, where of old were wont to be,
For the blind, the halt, and leper, alms and hospitality

---

* Teach Molaga—"The House of St. Molaga"—now called Timoleague. In Munster. Mangan has also translated this poem very finely According to him, the author was John O'Cullen, a native of Cork, who died in the year 1816.

Still the ancient seat was standing, built against the
 buttress gray,
Where the clergy used to welcome weary trav'llers on
 their way;
There I sat me down in sadness, 'neath my cheek I
 placed my hand,
Till the tears fell hot and briny down upon the grassy
 land

There, I said in woful sorrow, weeping bitterly the
 while,
Was a time when joy and gladness reigned within this
 ruined pile;—
Was a time when bells were tinkling, clergy preaching
 peace abroad,
Psalms a-singing, music ringing praises to the mighty
 God.

Empty aisle, deserted chancel, tower tottering to your
 fall,
Many a storm since then has beaten on the gray head of
 your wall!
Many a bitter storm and tempest has your roof-tree
 turned away,
Since you first were formed a temple to the Lord of
 night and day.

Holy house of ivied gables, that were once the country's
 boast,
Houseless now in weary wandering are you scattered,
 saintly host;
Lone you are to-day, and dismal,—joyful psalms no more
 are heard,
Where, within your choir, her vesper screeches the cat-
 headed bird.

Ivy from your eaves is growing, nettles round your
 green hearthstone,
Winds howl where, in your corners, dropping waters make
 their moan

Where the lark to early matins used your clergy forth to call,
There, alas! no tongue is stirring, save the daws upon the wall.

Refectory cold and empty, dormitory bleak and bare,
Where are now your pious uses, simple bed and frugal fare?
Gone your abbot, rule and order, broken down your altar stones;
Nought I see beneath your shelter, save a heap of clayey bones.

Oh! the hardship—oh! the hatred, tyranny, and cruel war,
Persecution and oppression that have left you as you are!
I myself once also prospered;—mine is, too, an altered plight;
Trouble, care, and age have left me good for nought but grief to-night.

Gone, my motion and my vigour,—gone, the use of eye and ear;
At my feet lie friends and children, powerless and corrupting here;
Wo is written on my visage, in a nut my heart would lie—
Death's deliverance were welcome—Father, let the old man die.

## AVONDHU.

### BY J. J. CALLANAN.

[Avondhu—The Blackwater, Avunduff of Spenser. There are several rivers of this name in the counties of Cork and Kerry, but the one
here mentioned is by far the most considerable. It rises in a mountain called Meenganine, in the latter county, and discharges itself in
the sea at Youghal. For the length of its course, and the beauty and
variety of scenery through which it flows, it is superior to any river in
Munster.]

Oh, Avondhu, I wish I were
As once upon that mountain bare,
Where thy young waters laugh and shine
On the wild breast of Meenganine.
I wish I were by Cleada's* hill,
Or by Glenruachra's rushy rill;
But no! I never more shall view
Those scenes I loved by Avondhu.

Farewell, ye soft and purple streaks
Of evening on the beauteous Reeks; †
Farewell ye mists, that loved to ride
On Cahirbearna's stormy side.
Farewell, November's moaning breeze,
Wild minstrel of the dying trees:
Clara! a fond farewell to you,
No more we meet by Avondhu.

No more—but thou, O glorious hill,
Lift to the moon thy forehead still;
Flow on, flow on, thou dark swift river,
Upon thy free wild course for ever.
Exult young hearts in lifetime's spring,
And taste the joys pure love can bring;
But wanderer go, they're not for you—
Farewell, farewell, sweet Avondhu.

* **Cleada** and Cahirbearna (the hill of the four gaps) form part o the
chain of mountains which stretches westward from Mill-street to
Killarney.
† Macgillcuddy's Reeks, in the neighbourhood of Killarney.

## THE ROCK OF CASHEL.

#### BY THE REV. DR. MURRAY.

Fair was that eve, as if from earth away
    All trace of sin and sorrow
Passed, in the light of the eternal day,
    That knows nor night nor morrow.

The pale and shadowy mountains, in the dim
    And glowing distance piled!
A sea of light along the horizon's rim,
    Unbroken, undefiled!

Blue sky, and cloud, and grove, and hill, and glen,
    The form and face of man
Beamed with unwonted beauty, as if then
    New earth and heaven bega

Yet heavy grief was on me, and I gazed
    On thee through gushing tears,
Thou relic of a glory that once blazed
    So bright in bygone years!

Wreck of a ruin! lovelier, holier far,
    Thy ghastly hues of death,
Than the cold forms of newer temples are—
    Shrines of a priestless faith.

In lust and rapine, treachery and blood,
    *Its* iron domes were built;
Darkly they frown, where God's own altars stood,
    In hatred and in guilt.

But to make thee, of loving hearts the love,
    Was coined to living stone;
Truth, peace, and piety together strove
    To form thee for their own.

And thou wast theirs, and they within thee met,
   And did thy presence fill;
And their sweet light, even while thine own is set,
   Hovers around thee still.

'Tis not the work of mind, or hand, or eye,
   Builder's or sculptor's skill,
Thy site, thy beauty, or thy majesty—
   Not these my bosom thrill.

'Tis that a glorious monument thou art,
   Of the true faith of old,
When faith was one in all the nation's heart,
   Purer than purest gold.

A light, when darkness on the nations dwelt,
   In Erin found a home—
The mind of Greece, the warm heart of the Celt,
   The bravery of Rome.

But O! the pearl, the gem, the glory of her youth,
   That shone upon her brow;
She clung for ever to the Chair of Truth—
   Clings to it now!

Love of my love, and temple of my God!
   How would I now clasp thee
Close to my heart, and, even as thou wast trod,
   So with thee trodden be!

O, for one hour a thousand years ago,
   Within thy precincts dim,
To hear the chant, in deep and measured flow,
   Of psalmody and hymn!

To see of priests the long and white array,
   Around thy silver shrines—
The people kneeling prostrate far away,
   In thick and chequer'd lines.

To see the Prince of Cashel o'er the rest,
    Their prelate and their king.
The sacred bread and chalice by him blest,
    Earth's holiest offering.

To hear, in piety's own Celtic tongue,
    The most heart-touching prayer
That fervent suppliants e'er was heard among,—
    O, to be then and there!

There was a time all this within thy walls
    Was felt, and heard, and seen;
Faint image only now thy sight recals
    Of all that once hath been.

The creedless, heartless, murderous robber came,
    And never since that time
Round thy torn altars burned the sacred flame,
    Or rose the chant sublime.

Thy glory in a crimson tide went down,
    Beneath the cloven hoof—
Altar and priest, mitre, and cope, and crown,
    And choir, and arch, and roof.

O, but to see thee, when thou wilt rise again—
    For thou again wilt rise,
And with the splendours of thy second reign
    Dazzle a nation's eyes!

Children of those who made thee what thou wast,
    Shall lift thee from the tomb,
And clothe thee, for the spoiling of the past,
    In more celestial bloom.

And psalm, and hymn, and gold, and precious stones
    And gems beyond all price,
And priest, and altar, o'er the martyr's bones,
    And daily sacrifice,

And endless prayer, and crucifix, and shrine,
   And all religion's dower,
And thronging worshippers shall yet be thine—
   O, but to see that hour!

And who shall smite thee then?—and who shall see
   Thy second glory o'er?
When they who make thee free themselves are free,
   To fall no more.

## LOCH INA.

A BEAUTIFUL SALT-WATER LAKE, IN THE COUNTY OF
CORK, NEAR BALTIMORE.

I know a lake where the cool waves break,
   And softly fall on the silver sand—
And no steps intrude on that solitude,
   And no voice, save mine, disturbs the strand.

And a mountain bold like a giant of old
   Turned to stone by some magic spell,
Uprears in might his misty height,
   And his craggy sides are wooded well.

In the midst doth smile a little Isle,
   And its verdure shames the emerald's green—
On its grassy side, in ruined pride,
   A castle of old is darkling seen.

On its lofty crest the wild crane's nest,
   In its halls the sheep good shelter find;
And the ivy shades where a hundred blades
   Were hung, when the owners in sleep reclined.

That chieftain of old could he now behold
   His lordly tower a shepherd's pen,
His corpse, long dead, from its narrow bed
   Would rise, with anger and shame again.

'Tis sweet to gaze when the sun's bright rays
  Are cooling themselves in the trembling wave—
But 'tis sweeter far when the evening star
  Shines like a smile at Friendship's grave.

There the hollow shells, through their wreathed cells,
  Make music on the silent shore,
As the summer breeze, through the distant trees,
  Murmurs in fragrant breathings o'er.

And the sea-weed shines, like the hidden mines
  Of the fairy cities beneath the sea;
And the wave-washed stones are bright as the thrones
  Of the ancient Kings of Araby.

If it were my lot in that fairy spot
  To live for ever, and dream 'twere mine,
Courts might woo, and kings pursue,
  Ere I would leave thee—Loved Loch-Ine.

## THE RETURNED EXILE.

### BY B. SIMMONS.

Blue Corrin! how softly the evening light goes,
Fading far o'er thy summit from ruby to rose,
As if loth to deprive the deep woodlands below
Of the love and the glory they drink in its glow:
Oh, home-looking Hill! how beloved dost thou rise
Once more to my sight through the shadowy skies,
Watching still, in thy sheltering grandeur unfurled,
The landscape to me that so long was the world.
Fair evening—blest evening! one moment delay
Till the tears of the Pilgrim are dried in thy ray—
Till he feels that through years of long absence, not one
Of his friends—the lone rock and gray ruin—is gone.

Not one :—as I wind the sheer fastnesses through,
The valley of boyhood is bright in my view!
Once again my glad spirit its fetterless flight
May wing through a sphere of unclouded delight,
O'er one maze of broad orchard, green meadow, and slope—
From whose tints I once pictured the pinions of hope;
Still the hamlet gleams white—still the church yews are weeping,
Where the sleep of the peaceful my fathers are sleeping;
The vane tells, as usual, its fib from the mill,
But the wheel tumbles loudly and merrily still,
And the tower of the Roches stands lonely as ever,
With its grim shadow rusting the gold of the river.

My own pleasant River, bloom-skirted, behold,
Now sleeping in shade, now refulgently rolled,
Where long through the landscape it tranquilly flows,
Scarcely breaking, Glen-coorah, thy glorious repose!
By the Park's lovely pathways it lingers and shines,
Where the cushat's low call, and the murmur of pines,
And the lips of the lily seem wooing its stay
'Mid their odorous dells;—but 'tis off and away,
Rushing out through the clustering oaks, in whose shade,
Like a bird in the branches, an arbour I made,
Where the blue eyes of Eve often closed o'er the book,
While I read of stout Sindbad, or voyaged with Cook.

Wild haunt of the Harper! I stand by thy spring,
Whose waters of silver still sparkle and fling
Their wealth at my feet,—and I catch the deep glow,
As in long-vanished hours, of the lilacs that blow
By the low cottage porch—and the same crescent moon
That then ploughed, like a pinnace, the purple of June,
Is white on Glen-duff, and all blooms as unchanged
As if years had not passed since thy greenwood I ranged—
As if ONE were not fled, who imparted a soul
Of divinest enchantment and grace to the whole,
Whose being was bright as that fair moon above,
And all deep and all pure as thy waters her love.

Thou long-vanished Angel! whose faithfulness threw
O'er my gloomy existence one glorified hue!
Dost thou still, as of yore, when the evening grows
    dim.,
And the blackbird by Downing is hushing its hymn,
Remember the bower by the Funcheon's blue side
Where the whispers were soft as the kiss of the tide?
Dost thou still think, with pity and peace on thy brow,
Of him who, toil-harassed and time-shaken now,
While the last light of day, like his hopes, has departed,
On the turf thou hast hallowed, sinks down weary-
    hearted,
And calls on thy name, and the night-breeze that sighs
Through the boughs that once blest thee is all that
    replies?

But thy summit, far Corrin, is fading in gray,
And the moonlight grows mellow on lonely Cloughlea;
And the laugh of the young, as they loiter about
Through the elm-shaded alleys, rings joyously out:
Happy souls! they have yet the dark chalice to taste,
And like others to wander life's desolate waste—
To hold wassail with sin, or keep vigil with woe;
But the same fount of yearning, wherever they go,
Welling up in their heart-depths, to turn at the last
(As the stag when the barb in his bosom is fast)
To their lair in the hills, on their childhood that rose
And find the sole blessing I seek for—REPOSE!

## GLENFINISHK.*

### BY JOSEPH O'LEARY.

GLENFINISHK! where thy waters mix with Araglen's
    wild tide,
'Tis sweet, at hush of evening, to wander by thy side!

* Glenfinishk (the glen of the fair waters), in the county of Cork.

'Tis sweet to hear the night-winds sigh along Macrona's
    wood,
And mingle their wild music with the murmur of thy
    flood!

'Tis sweet, when in the deep blue vault the morn is shin-
    ing bright,
To watch where thy clear waters are breaking into light;
To mark the starry sparks that o'er thy smoother surface
    gleam,
As if some fairy hand were flinging diamonds on thy
    stream!

Oh! if departed spirits e'er to this dark world return,
'Tis in some lonely, lovely spot like this they would so-
    journ;
Whate'er their mystic rites may be, no human eye is
    here,
Save mine, to mark their mystery—no human voice is
    near.

At such an hour, in such a scene, I could forget my
    birth—
I could forget I e'er have been, or am, a thing of earth;
Shake off the fleshly bonds that hold my soul in thrall,
    and be
Even like themselves, a spirit, as boundless and as free!

Ye shadowy race! if we believe the tales of legends old,
Ye sometimes hold high converse with those of mortal
    mould:
Oh! come, whilst now my soul is free, and bear me in
    your train,
Ne'er to return to misery and this dark world again!

## THE MOUNTAIN FERN.

**BY THE AUTHOR OF "THE MONKS OF KILCREA."**

Oh, the Fern! the Fern!—the Irish hill Fern!—
That girds our blue lakes from Lough Ine * to Lough Erne,
That waves on our crags, like the plume of a king,
And bends, like a nun, over clear well and spring !
The fairy's tall palm tree! the heath bird's fresh nest,
And the couch the red deer deems the sweetest and best,
With the free winds to fan it, and dew drops to gem,—
Oh, what can ye match with its beautiful stem ?
From the shrine of Saint Finbar, by lone Avonbuie,
To the halls of Dunluce, with its towers by the sea,
From the hill of Knockthu to the rath of Moyvore,
Like a chaplet it circles our green island o'er,—
In the bawn of the chief, by the anchorite's cell,
On the hill top, or greenwood, by streamlet or well,
With a spell on each leaf, which no mortal can learn †—
Oh, there never was plant like the Irish hill Fern !

Oh, the Fern! the Fern!—the Irish hill Fern!—
That shelters the weary, or wild roe, or kern.
Thro' the glens of Kilcoe rose a shout on the gale,
As the Saxons rushed forth, in their wrath, from the Pale,
With bandog and bloodhound, all savage to see,
To hunt thro' Clunealla the wild Rapparee !
Hark! a cry from yon dell on the startled ear rings,
And forth from the wood the young fugitive springs,
Thro' the copse, o'er the bog, and, oh, saints be his guide !
His fleet step now falters—there's blood on his side—
Yet onward he strains, climbs the cliff, fords the stream
And sinks on the hill top, mid brachen leaves green,

---

* Lough Ine, a singularly romantic lake in the western mountains of Cork; of Lough Erne, I hope to Irishmen it is unnecessary to speak.
† The fortunate discoverer of the fern seed is supposed to obtain the power of rendering himself invisible at pleasure.

And thick o'er his brow are their fresh clusters piled,
And they cover his form, as a mother her child;
And the Saxon is baffled!—they never discern
Where it shelters and saves him—the Irish hill **Fern!**

Oh, the Fern! the Fern!—the Irish hill Fern!—
That pours a wild keen o'er the hero's gray cairn;
Go, hear it at midnight, when stars are all out,
And the wind o'er the hill side is moaning about,
With a rustle and stir, and a low wailing tone
That thrills thro' the heart with its whispering lone,
And ponder its meaning, when haply you stray
Where the halls of the stranger in ruin decay.
With night owls for warders, the goshawk for guest,
And their dais* of honor by cattle-hoofs prest—
With its fosse choked with rushes, and spider-webs flung,
Over walls where the marchmen their red weapons hung,
With a curse on their name, and a sigh for the hour
That tarries so long—look! what waves on the tower?
With an omen and sign, and an augury stern,
'Tis the *Green Flag* of Time!—'tis the Irish hill Fern!

---

## ADARE.†

### BY GERALD GRIFFIN.

Oh, sweet Adare! oh, lovely vale!
  Oh, soft retreat of sylvan splendour!
Nor summer sun, nor morning gale
  E'er hailed a scene more softly tender.

* The dais was an elevated portion of the great hall or dining-room, set apart in feudal times for those of gentle blood, and was, in consequence, regarded with peculiar feelings of veneration and respect.
† This beautiful and interesting locality is about eight miles from Limerick.

How shall I tell the thousand charms
   Within thy verdant bosom dwelling,
Where, lulled in Nature's fost'ring arms,
   Soft peace abides and joy excelling!

Ye morning airs, how sweet at dawn
   The slumbering boughs your song awaken,
Or linger o'er the silent lawn,
   With odour of the harebell taken.
Thou rising sun, how richly gleams
   Thy smile from far Knockfierna's mountain,
O'er waving woods and bounding streams,
   And many a grove and glancing fountain.

Ye clouds of noon, how freshly there,
   When summer heats the open meadows,
O'er parched hill and valley fair,
   All cooly lie your veiling shadows.
Ye rolling shades and vapours gray,
   Slow creeping o'er the golden heaven,
How soft ye seal the eye of day,
   And wreath the dusky brow of even.

In sweet Adare, the jocund spring
   His notes of odorous joy is breathing,
The wild birds in the woodland sing,
   The wild flowers in the vale are breathing.
There winds the Mague, as silver clear,
   Among the elms so sweetly flowing,
There fragrant in the early year,
   Wild roses on the banks are blowing.

The wild duck seeks the sedgy bank,
   Or dives beneath the glistening billow.
Where graceful droop and clustering dank
   The osier bright and rustling willow.
The hawthorn scents the leafy dale,
   In thicket lone the stag is belling,
And sweet along the echoing vale
   The sound of vernal joy is swelling.

## THE VALE OF SHANGANAH.

### BY D. F. M'CARTHY.

[By the "Vale of Shanganah," I understand the entire of that beautiful panorama which stretches out from the foot of Killiney Hill to Bray Head, and from the "White Strand" to the Sugar Loaf Mountains. Few inhabitants of Dublin require to be informed that the ancient Irish name of these picturesque mountains is a word which means "The Golden Spears," and that by *Ben Heder* is meant the Hill of Howth.]

WHEN I have knelt in the Temple of Duty,
Worshipping honour and valour and beauty—
When, like a brave man, in fearless resistance,
I have fought the good fight on the field of existence;
When a home I have won by a long life of labour,
By the thoughts of my soul or the steel of my sabre—
Be that home a calm home where my old age may
　　rally,
A home full of peace in this sweet pleasant valley.
　　Sweetest of vales is the Vale of Shanganah!
　　Greenest of vales is the Vale of Shanganah!
　　May the accents of love, like the droppings of
　　　manna,
　　Fall sweet on my heart in the Vale of Shanganah!

Fair is this isle—this dear child of the ocean—
Nurtured with more than a mother's devotion;
For see! in what rich robes has Nature arrayed her,
From the waves of the west to the cliffs of *Ben Heder*,
By Glengariff's lone islets—Loch Lene's fairy water,
So lovely was each, that then matchless I thought her;
But I feel, as I stray through each sweet-scented ailey,
Less wild but more fair is this soft verdant valley!
　　Sweetest of vales is the Vale of Shanganah!
　　Greenest of vales is the Vale of Shanganah!
　　No wide-spreading prairie—no Indian savanna,
　　So dear to the eye as the Vale of Shanganah!

How pleased, how delighted, the rapt eye reposes
On the picture of beauty this valley discloses,
From that margin of silver, whereon the blue water
Doth glance like the eyes of the ocean foam's daughter!
To where, with the red clouds of morning combining,
The tall "Golden Spears" o'er the mountains are shining,
With the hue of their heather, as sunlight advances,
Like purple flags furled round the staffs of the lances!
 Sweetest of vales is the Vale of Shanganah!
 Greenest of vales is the Vale of Shanganah!
 No lands far away by the calm Susquehannah,
 So tranquil and fair as the Vale of Shanganah!

But here, even here the lone heart were benighted,
No beauty could reach it, if love did not light it;
'Tis that makes the Earth, oh! what mortal can doubt it?
A garden with *it*—but a desert without it!
With the lov'd one, to whom, thoughtful feeling doth teach her,
That goodness of heart makes the beauty of feature '
How glad, through this vale, would I float down life's river,
Enjoying God's bounty, and blessing the Giver!
 Sweetest of vales is the Vale of Shanganah!
 Greenest of vales is the Vale of Shanganah!
 May the accents of love, like the droppings of manna,
 Fall sweet on my heart in the Vale of Shanganah!

## DEIRDRE'S FAREWELL TO ALBA.[a]

#### BY SAMUEL FERGUSON, M.R.I.A.

FAREWELL to fair Alba, high house of the sun,
Farewell to the mountain, the cliff, and the dun;
Dun Sweeny adieu! for my love cannot stay,
And tarry I may not when love cries away.

Glen Vashan! Glen Vashan! where roe-bucks run free,
Where my love used to feast on the red deer with me,
Where rocked on thy waters while stormy winds blew
My love used to slumber, Glen Vashan adieu!

Glendaro! Glendaro! where birchen boughs weep
Honey dew at high noon o'er the nightingale's sleep,
Where my love used to lead me to hear the cuckoo
Mong the high hazel bushes, Glendaro, adieu!

Glen Urchy! Glen Urchy! where loudly and long
My love used to wake up the woods with his song,
While the son of the rock, from the depths of the dell,
Laughed sweetly in answer, Glen Urchy, farewell!

Glen Etive! Glen Etive! where dappled does roam,
Where I leave the green sheeling I first called a home
Where with me and my true love delighted to dwell,
The sun made his mansion, Glen Etive, farewell!

Farewell to Inch Draynach, adieu to the roar
Of the blue billows bursting in light on the shore;
Dun Fiagh, farewell! for my love cannot stay,
And tarry I may not when love cries away.

[a] Scotland.

## A SIGH FOR KNOCKMANY.

### BY WILLIAM CARLETON.

Take, proud ambition, take thy fill
   Of pleasures won through toil or crime;
Go, learning, climb thy rugged hill,
   And give thy name to future time:
Philosophy, be keen to see
   Whate'er is just, or false, or vain,
Take each thy meed, but, oh! give me
   To range my mountain glens again.


Pure was the breeze that fann'd my cheek,
   As o'er Knockmany's brow I went;
When every lonely dell could speak
   In airy music, vision sent:
False world, I hate thy cares and thee,
   I hate the treacherous haunts of men;
Give back my early heart to me,
   Give back to me my mountain glen.


How light my youthful visions shone,
   When spann'd by fancy's radiant form;
But now her glittering bow is gone,
   And leaves me but the cloud and storm.
With wasted form, and cheek all pale—
   With heart long scared by grief and pain;
Dunroe, I'll seek thy native gale,
   I'll tread my mountain glens again.


Thy breeze once more may fan my blood,
   Thy vallies all, are lovely still;
And I may stand, where oft I stood,
   In lonely musings on thy hill.

But ah! the spell is gone;—no art
  In crowded town, or native plain,
Can teach a crush'd and breaking heart
  To pipe the song of youth again.

---

## TIPPERARY.

Were you ever in sweet Tipperary, where the fields are
    so sunny and green,
And the heath-brown Slieve-bloom and the Galtees look
    down with so proud a mien?
'Tis there you would see more beauty than is on all
    Irish ground—
God bless you, my sweet Tipperary, for where could
    your match be found?

They say that your hand is fearful, that darkness is in
    your eye:
But I'll not let them dare to talk so black and bitter a
    lie.
Oh! no, *macushla storin!* bright, bright, and warm are
    you,
With hearts as bold as the men of old, to yourselves and
    your country true.

And when there is gloom upon you, bid them think who
    has brought it there—
Sure a frown or a word of hatred was not made for your
    face so fair;
You've a hand for the grasp of friendship—another to
    make them quake,
And they're welcome to whichsoever it pleases them
    most to take.

Shall our homes, like the huts of Connaught, be crumbled before our eyes?
Shall we fly; like a flock of wild geese, from all that we love and prize?
No! by those who were here before us, no churl shall our tyrant be;
Our land it is theirs by plunder, but, by Brigid, ourselves are free.

No! we do not forget the greatness did once to sweet Eire belong;
No treason or craven spirit was ever our race among;
And no frown or no word of hatred we give--but to pay them back;
In evil we only follow our enemies' darksome track.

Oh! come for a while among us, and give us the friendly hand;
And you'll see that old Tipperary is a loving and gladsome land;
From Upper to Lower Ormond, bright welcomes and smiles will spring--
On the plains of Tipperary the stranger is like a king.

# LEGENDARY BALLADS.

## THE WELSHMEN OF TIRAWLEY.

### BY SAMUEL FERGUSON, M.R.I.A.

[Several Welsh families, associates in the invasion of Strongbow, settled in the west of Ireland. Of these, the principal whose names have been preserved by the Irish antiquarians were the Walshes, Joyces, Heils (*a quibus* MacIlale), Lawlesses, Tolmyns, Lynotts, and Barretts, which last draw their pedigree from Walynus, son of Gnyndally, the *Ard Maor*, or High Steward of the Lordship of Camelot, and had their chief seats in the territory of the two Bacs, in the barony of Tirawley, and county of Mayo. *Cloghan-an-n'dall*, or "the Blind Men's Stepping-stones," are still pointed out on the Duvowen river, about four miles north of Crossmolina, in the townland of Garranard; and *Tubber na Scorney*, or "Scrag's Well," in the opposite townland of Carns, in the same barony. For a curious *terrier* or applotment of the Mac William's revenue, as acquired under the circumstances stated in the legend preserved by Mac Firbis, see Mr. O'Donovan's highly-learned and interesting "Genealogies, &c. of Hy Fiachrach," in the publications of the *Irish Archæological Society*—a great monument of antiquarian and topographical erudition.]

SCORNEY BWEE, the Barretts' bailiff, lewd and lame,
To lift the Lynott's taxes when he came,
Rudely drew a young maid to him;
Then the Lynotts rose and slew him,
And in Tubber-na-Scorney threw him—
   Small your blame,
   Sons of Lynott!
Sing the vengeance of the Welshmen of Tirawley.

Then the Barretts to the Lynotts gave a choice,
Saying, "Hear, ye murderous brood, men and boys,
Choose ye now, without delay,
Will ye lose your eyesight, say,
Or your manhoods, here to-day?"
    Sad your choice,
    Sons of Lynott!
Sing the vengeance of the Welshmen of Tirawley.

Then the little boys of the Lynotts, weeping, said,
"Only leave us our eyesight in our head."
But the bearded Lynotts then
Quickly answered back again,
"Take our eyes, but leave us men,
    Alive or dead,
    Sons of Wattin!"
Sing the vengeance of the Welshmen of Tirawley.

So the Barretts, with sewing-needles sharp and smooth,
Let the light out of the eyes of every youth,
And of every bearded man
Of the broken Lynott clan;
Then their darkened faces wan
    Turning south
    To the river—.
Sing the vengeance of the Welshmen of Tirawley.

O'er the slippery stepping-stones of Clochan-a-n'dall
They drove them, laughing loud at every fall,
As their wandering footsteps dark
Failed to reach the slippery mark,
And the swift stream swallowed stark,
    One and all,
    As they stumbled—
Sing the vengeance of the Welshmen of Tirawley.

Out of all the blinded Lynotts, one alone
Walked erect from stepping-stone to stone;
So back again they brought you,
And a second time they wrought you

With their needles; but never got you
        Once to groan,
        Emon Lynott,
For the vengeance of the Welshmen of Tirawley.

But with prompt-projected footsteps sure as ever,
Emon Lynott again crossed the river,
Though Duvowen was rising fast,
And the shaking stones o'ercast
By cold floods boiling past;
        Yet you never,
        Emon Lynott,
Faltered once before your foemen of Tirawley!

But, turning on Ballintubber bank, you stood,
And the Barretts thus bespoke o'er the flood—
"Oh, ye foolish sons of Wattin,
Small amends are these you've gotten,
For, while Scorney Bwee lies rotten,
        I am good
        For vengeance!"
Sing the vengeance of the Welshmen of Tirawley.

"For 'tis neither in eye nor eyesight that a man
Bears the fortunes of himself or of his clan;
But in the manly mind
And in loins with vengeance lined,
That your needles could never find,
        Though they ran
        Through my heartstrings!"
Sing the vengeance of the Welshmen of Tirawley.

"But, little your women's needles do I reck;
For the night from heaven never fell so black,
But Tirawley, and abroad
From the Moy to Cuan-an-fod,
I could walk it every sod,
        Path and track,
        Ford and togher,
Seeking vengeance on you, Barretts of Tirawley!

"The night when Dathy O'Dowda broke your camp,
What Barrett among you was it held the lamp—
Showed the way to those two feet,
When through wintry wind and sleet,
I guided your blind retreat
    In the swamp
    Of Beäl-an-asa?
O ye vengeance-destined ingrates of Tirawley!"

So leaving loud-shriek-echoing Garranard,
The Lynott like a red dog hunted hard,
With his wife and children seven,
'Mong the beasts and fowls of heaven
In the hollows of Glen Nephin,
    Light-debarred,
    Made his dwelling,
Planning vengeance on the Barretts of Tirawley.

And ere the bright-orb'd year its course had run,
On his brown round-knotted knee he nursed a son,
A child of light, with eyes
As clear as are the skies
In summer, when sunrise
    Has begun;
    So the Lynott
Nursed his vengeance on the Barretts of Tirawley

And, as ever the bright boy grew in strength and size,
Made him perfect in each manly exercise,
The salmon in the flood,
The dun deer in the wood,
The eagle in the cloud
    To surprise,
    On Ben Nephin,
Far above the foggy fields of Tirawley.

With the yellow-knotted spear-shaft, with the bow,
With the steel, prompt to deal shot and blow,
He taught him from year to year
And trained him, without a peer,

For a perfect cavalier,
   Hoping so—
     Far his forethought—
For vengeance on the Barretts of Tirawley.

And, when mounted on his proud-bounding steed,
Emon Oge sat a cavalier indeed;
Like the ear upon the wheat
When winds in autumn beat
On the bending stems, his seat;
   And the speed
    Of his courser
Was the wind from Barna-na-gee o'er Tirawley!

Now when fifteen sunny summers thus were spent,
(He perfected in all accomplishment)—
The Lynott said, "My child,
We are over long exiled
From mankind in this wild—
   —Time we went
    O'er the mountain
To the countries lying over-against Tirawley."

So out over mountain-moors, and mosses brown,
And green stream-gathering vales, they journeyed
  down;
Till, shining like a star,
Through the dusky gleams afar,
The bailey of Castlebar,
   And the town
    Of Mac William
Rose bright before the wanderers of Tirawley.

"Look southward, my boy, and tell me as we go,
What seest thou by the loch-head below."
"Oh, a stone-house strong and great,
And a horse-host at the gate,
And their captain in armour of plate—
   Grand the show!
    Great the glancing!
High the heroes of this land below Tirawley!

" And a beautiful Bantierna by his side,
Yellow gold on all her gown-sleeves wide;
And in her hand a pearl
Of a young, little, fair-haired girl——
Said the Lynott, "It is the Earl!
   Let us ride
   To his presence."
And before him came the exiles of Tirawley.

"God save thee, MacWilliam," the Lynott thus began;
" God save all here besides of this clan;
For gossips dear to me
Are all in company—
For in these four bones ye see
   A kindly man
   Of the Britons—
Emon Lynott of Garranard of Tirawley.

" And hither, as kindly gossip-law allows,
I come to claim a scion of thy house
To foster ; for thy race,
Since William Conquer's* days,
Have ever been wont to place,
   With some spouse
   Of a Briton,
A MacWilliam Oge, to foster in Tirawley.

" And to show thee in what sort our youth are taught,
I have hither to thy home of valour brought
This one son of my age,
For a sample and a pledge
For the equal tutelage,
   In right thought,
   Word, and action,
Of whatever son ye give into Tirawley."

When MacWilliam beheld the brave boy ride and run,
Saw the spear-shaft from his white shoulder spun—

---

* William Fitz Adelm de Burgho, the conqueror of

With a sigh, and with a smile,
He said,—" I would give the spoil
Of a county, that Tibbot Moyle,
   My own son,
    Were accomplished
Like this branch of the kindly Britons of Tirawley "


When the Lady MacWilliam she heard him speak
And saw the ruddy roses on his cheek,
She said, " I would give a purse
Of red gold to the nurse
That would rear my Tibbot no worse;
   But I seek
    Hitherto vainly—
Heaven grant that I now have found her in Tirawley!"


So they said to the Lynott, "Here, take our bird!
And as pledge for the keeping of thy word,
Let this scion here remain
Till thou comest back again:
Meanwhile the fitting train
   Of a lord
    Shall attend thee
With the lordly heir of Connaught into Tirawley."


So back to strong-throng-gathering Garranard,
Like a lord of the country with his guard,
Came the Lynott, before them all.
Once again over Clochan-an'-dall,
Steady-striding, erect, and tall,
   And his ward
    On his shoulders;
To the wonder of the Welshman of Tirawley.


Then a diligent foster-father you would deem
The Lynott, teaching Tibbot, by mead and stream,
To cast the spear, to ride,
To stem the rushing tide,

With what feats of body beside,
          Might beseem
      A Mac William,
Fostered free among the Welshmen of Tirawley.

But the lesson of hell he taught him in heart and mind,
For to what desire soever he inclined,
Of anger, lust, or pride,
He had it gratified,
Till he ranged the circle wide
          Of a blind
      Self-indulgence,
Ere he came to youthful manhood in Tirawley.

Then, even as when a hunter slips a hound,
Lynott loosed him—God's leashes all unbound—
In the pride of power and station,
And the strength of youthful passion,
On the daughters of thy nation,
          All around,
      Wattin Barrett!
Oh! the vengeance of the Welshmen of Tirawley!

Bitter grief and burning anger, rage and shame,
Filled the houses of the Barretts where'er he came;
Till the young men of the Bac
Drew by night upon his track,
And slew him at Cornassack—
          Small your blame,
      Sons of Wattin!
Sing the vengeance of the Welshmen of Tirawley.

Said the Lynott, "The day of my vengeance is drawing near,
The day for which, through many a long dark year,
I have toiled through grief and sin—
Call ye now the Brehons in,
And let the plea begin
          Over the bier
      Of Mac William,
For an eric upon the Barretts of Tirawley."

Then the Brehons to Mac William Burk decreed
An eric upon Clan Barrett for the deed;
And the Lynott's share of the fine,
As foster-father, was nine
Ploughlands and nine score kine;
   But no need
   Had the Lynott,
Neither care, for land or cattle in Tirawley.

But rising, while all sat silent on the spot,
He said, "The law says—doth it not?—
If the foster-sire elect
His portion to reject,
He may then the right exact
   To applot
   The short eric."
"'Tis the law," replied the Brehons of Tirawley.

Said the Lynott, "I once before had a choice
Proposed me, wherein law had little voice;
But now I choose, and say,
As lawfully I may,
I applot the mulct to-day;
   So rejoice
   In your ploughlands
And your cattle which I renounce throughout Tirawley

"And thus I applot the mulct: I divide
The land throughout Clan Barrett on every side
Equally, that no place
May be without the face
Of a foe of Wattin's race—
   That the pride
   Of the Barretts
May be humbled hence for ever throughout Tirawley.

"I adjudge a seat in every Barrett's hall
To Mac William: in every stable I give a stall

To Mac William: and, beside,
Whenever a Burk shall ride
Through Tirawley, I provide
   At his call
    Needful grooming,
Without charge from any Brughaidh of Tirawley.

"Thus lawfully I avenge me for the throes
Ye lawlessly caused me and caused those
Unhappy shamefaced ones,
Who, their mothers expected once,
Would have been the sires of sons—
   O'er whose woes
    Often weeping,
I have groaned in my exile from Tirawley.

" I demand not of you your manhoods; but I take—
For the Burks will take it—your Freedom! for the sake
Of which all manhood's given
And all good under heaven,
And, without which, better even
   Ye should make
    Yourselves barren,
Than see your children slaves throughout Tirawley!

"Neither take I your eyesight from you; as you took
Mine and ours: I would have you daily look
On one another's eyes,
When the strangers tyrannize
By your hearths, and blushes arise.
   That ye brook
    Without vengeance
The insults of troops of Tibbots throughout Tirawley!

" The vengeance I designed, now is done.
And the days of me and mine nearly run.—
For, for this, I have broken faith,
Teaching him who lies beneath

This pall, to merit death;
          And my son
            To his father
Stands pledged for other teaching in Tirawley."

Said Mac William—" Father and son, hang those high!"
And the Lynott they hanged speedily;
But across the salt-sea water,
To Scotland with the daughter
Of Mac William—well you got her!—
          Did you fly,
            Edmund Lindsay,
The gentlest of all the Welshmen of Tirawley!

'Tis thus the ancient Ollaves of Erin tell
How, through lewdness and revenge, it befel
That the sons of William Conquer
Came over the sons of Wattin,
Throughout all the bounds and borders
Of the land of Auley Mac Fiachra;
Till the Saxon Oliver Cromwell
And his valiant, Bible-guided,
Free heretics of Clan London
Coming in, in their succession,
Rooted out both Burk and Barrett,
And in their empty places
New stems of freedom planted,
With many a goodly sapling
Of manliness and virtue;
Which while their children cherish.
Kindly Irish of the Irish,
Neither Saxons nor Italians,
May the mighty God of Freedom
          Speed them well.
          Never taking
Further vengeance on his people of Tirawley.

## THE OUTLAW OF LOCH LENE.

#### BY J. J. CALLANAN.

O many a day have I made good ale in the glen,
That came not of stream, or malt;—like the brewing of men.
My bed was the ground; my roof, the greenwood above,
And the wealth that I sought one far kind glance from my love.

Alas! on that night when the horses I drove from the field,
That I was not near from terror my angel to shield.
She stretched forth her arms,—her mantle she flung to the wind,
And swam o'er Loch Lene, her outlawed lover to find.

O would that a freezing sleet-wing'd tempest did sweep,
And I and my love were alone, far off on the deep;
I'd ask not a ship, or a bark, or pinnace, to save,—
With her hand round my waist, I'd fear not the wind or the wave.

'Tis down by the lake where the wild tree fringes its sides,
The maid of my heart, my fair one of Heaven resides;—
I think as at eve she wanders its mazes along,
The birds go to sleep by the sweet wild twist of her song.

## AILEEN THE HUNTRESS.

### BY EDWARD WALSH.

[The incident related in the following ballad happened about the year 1731. Aileen, or Ellen, was daughter of M'Cartie, of Clidane, an estate originally bestowed upon this respectable branch of the family of M'Cartic More, by James, the seventh Earl of Desmond, and which, passing safe through the confiscations of Elizabeth, Cromwell, and William, remained in their possession until the beginning of the present century. Aileen, who is celebrated in the traditions of the people for her love of hunting, was the wife of James O'Connor, of Cluain-Tairbh, grandson of David, the founder of the *Siol-t Da*, a well-known sept at this day in Kerry. This David was grandson to Thomas MacTeige O'Connor, of Ahalahanna, head of the second house of O'Connor Kerry, who, forfeiting in 1666, escaped destruction by taking shelter among his relations, the Nagles of Monanimy.]

FAIR Aileen M'Cartie, O'Connor's young bride,
Forsakes her white pillow with matronly pride,
And calls forth her maidens (their number was nine)
To the bawn of her mansion, a-milking the kine.

They came at her bidding, in kirtle and gown,
And braided hair, jetty, and golden, and brown,
And form like the palm-tree, and step like the fawn,
And bloom like the wild rose that circled the bawn.

As the Guebre's round tower o'er the fane of Ardfert—
As the white hind of Brandon by young roes begirt—
As the moon in her glory 'mid bright stars outhung—
Stood Aileen M'Cartie her maidens among.

Beneath the rich kerchief, which matrons may wear,
Stray'd ringleted tresses of beautiful hair;
They wav'd on her fair neck, as darkly as though
'Twere the raven's wing shining o'er Mangerton's snow!

A circlet of pearls o'er her white bosom lay,
Erst worn by thy proud Queen, O'Connor the gay,*

* O'Connor, surnamed "*Sugach*," or the Gay, was a celebrated chief of this race, who flourished in the fifteenth century.

And now to the beautiful Aileen come down,
The rarest that ever shed light in the Laune.\*

The many-fring'd *falluinn*† that floated behind,
Gave its hues to the sun-light, its folds to the wind—
The brooch that refrain'd it some forefather bold
Had torn from a sea-king in battle-field old!

Around her went bounding two wolf-dogs of speed,
So tall in their stature, so pure in their breed;
While the maidens awake to the new-milk's soft fall
A song of O'Connor in Carraig's proud hall.

As the milk came outpouring, and the song came out-
  sung,
O'er the wall 'mid the maidens a red-deer out-sprung—
Then cheer'd the fair lady—then rush'd the mad hound—
And away with the wild stag in air-lifted bound!

The gem-fasten'd *falluinn* is dash'd on the bawn—
One spring o'er the tall fence—and Aileen is gone!
But morning's rous'd echoes to the deep dells proclaim
The course of that wild stag, the dogs, and the dame!

By Cluain Tairbh's green border, o'er moorland and
  height,
The red-deer shapes downward the rush of his flight—
In sunlight his antlers all gloriously flash,
And onward the wolf-dogs and fair huntress dash!

By Sliabh-Mis now winding, (rare hunting I ween!)
He gains the dark valley of Scota the queen‡

---

\* The river Laune flows from the Lakes of Killarney, and the cele
brated Kerry Pearls are found in its waters.
† "Fulluinn"—The Irish mantle.
‡ The first battle fought between the Milesians and the Tuatha de
Danans for the empire of Ireland was at Sliabh-Mis, in Kerry, in which
Scota, an Egyptian princess, and the relict of Milesius, was slain. A
valley on the north side of Sliabh-Mis, called Glean Scoithin, or the vale
of Scota, is said to be the place of her interment. The ancient chro
nicles assert that this battle was fought 1300 years before the Christian
era.

Who found in its bosom a cairn-lifted grave,
When Sliabh-Mis first flow'd with the blood of the
  brave!

By Coill-Cuaigh's* green shelter, the hollow rocks
  ring—
Coill-Cuaigh, of the cuckoo's first song in the spring,
Coill-Cuaigh of the tall oak and gale-scenting spray—
God's curse on the tyrants that wrought thy decay!

Now Maing's lovely border is gloriously won,
Now the towers of the island† gleam bright in the sun,
And now Ceall-an Amanach's‡ portals are pass'd,
Where headless the Desmond found refuge at last!

By Ard-na gcreach§ mountain, and Avonmore's head,
To the Earl's proud pavilion the panting deer fled—
Where Desmond's tall clansmen spread banners of pride,
And rush'd to the battle, and gloriously died!

The huntress is coming, slow, breathless, and pale,
Her raven locks streaming all wild in the gale;
She stops—and the breezes bring balm to her brow—
But wolf-dog and wild deer, oh! where are they now?

On Réidhlán-Tigh-an-Eárla, by Avonmore's well,
His bounding heart broken, the hunted deer fell,

---

\* "Coill-Cuaigh"--*The Wood of the Cuckoo*, so called from being the favourite haunt of the bird of summer, is now a bleak desolate moor. The axe of the stranger laid its honors low.

† "Castle Island" or the "Island of Kerry"—The stronghold of the Fitzgeralds.

‡ It was in this churchyard that the headless remains of the unfortunate Gerald, the 16th Earl of Desmond. were privately interred. The head was carefully pickled, and sent over to the English queen, who had it fixed on London-bridge. This mighty chieftain possessed more than 570,000 acres of land, and had a train of 500 gentlemen of his own name and race. At the source of the Blackwater, where he sought refuge from his inexorable foes, is a mountain called "Reidhlan Tigh-an-Earla," or "The Plain of the Earl's House." He was slain near Castle Island on 11th November, 1583.

§ "Ard-na gcreach"—The height of the spoils or armies.

And o'er him the brave hounds all gallantly died,
In death still victorious—their fangs in his side!

'Tis evening—the breezes beat cold on her breast,
And Aileen must seek her far home in the west;
Yet weeping, she lingers where the mist-wreathes are chill,
O'er the red-deer and tall dogs that lie on the hill!

Whose harp at the banquet told distant and wide,
This feat of fair Aileen, O'Connor's young bride?
O'Daly's—whose guerdon tradition hath told,
Was a purple-crown'd wine-cup of beautiful gold!

## SHANE DYMAS' DAUGHTER.

It was the eve of holy St. Bride,
  The Abbey bells were ringing,
And the meek-eyed nuns at eventide
  The vesper hymns were singing.

Alone, by the well of good St. Bride,
  A novice fair was kneeling;
And there seem'd not o'er her soul to glide
  One "shade of earthly feeling."

For ne'er did that clear and sainted well
  Reflect, from its crystal water,
A form more fair than the shadow that fell
  From O'Niall's lovely daughter.

Her eye was bright as the blue concave,
  And beaming with devotion;
Her bosom fair as the foam on the wave
  Of Erin's rolling ocean.

Yet O! forgive her that starting tear;
From home and kindred riven,
Fair Kathleen, many a long, long year,
Must be the Bride of Heaven.

Her beads were told, and the moonlight shone
Sweetly on Callan Water,
When her path was cross'd by a holy nun;—
"Benedicite, fair daughter!"

Fair Kathleen started—well did she know—
O what will not love discover!
Her country's scourge, and her father's foe,—
'Twas the voice of her Saxon lover.

"Raymond!"—"Oh hush, my Kathleen dear,
My path's beset with danger;
But cast not, love, those looks of fear
Upon thy dark-hair'd stranger.

"My red roan steed's in yon Culdee grove,
My bark is out at sea, love!
My boat is moored in the ocean cove;
Then haste away with me, love!

"My father has sworn my hand shall be
To Sidney's daughter given;
And thine, to-morrow, will offer thee
A sacrifice to heaven.

"But away, my love, away with me!
The breeze to the west is blowing;
And thither, across the dark-blue sea,
Are England's bravest going.*

"To a land where the breeze from the orange bowers
Comes over the exile's sorrow,

* Alluding to the settlement of Virginia by Sir Walter Raleigh.

Like the light-wing'd dreams of his early hours,
  Or his hope of a happier morrow.

" And there, in some valley's loneliness,
  By wood and mountain shaded,
We'll live in the light of wedded bliss,
  Till the lamp of life be faded.

" Then thither with me, my Kathleen, fly!
  The storms of life we'll weather,
Till in bliss beneath the western sky,
  We live, love, die together!"—

"Die, Saxon, now!"—At that fiend-like yell
  An hundred swords are gleaming:
Down the bubbling stream, from the tainted well,
  His heart's best blood is streaming.

In vain does he doff the hood so white,
  And vain his falchion flashing:
Five murderous brands through his corslet bright
  Within his heart are clashing!

His last groan echoing through the grove,
  His life blood on the water,
He dies,—thy first and thy only love,
  O'Niall's hapless daughter!

Vain, vain, was the shield of that breast of snow!
  In vain that eye beseech'd them;
Through his Kathleen's heart, the murderous blow
  Too deadly aimed, has reach'd him.

The spirit fled with the red red blood
  Fast gushing from her bosom;
The blast of death has blighted the bud
  Of Erin's loveliest blossom!

    \*    \*    \*    \*

'Tis morn ;—in the deepest doubt and dread
  The gloomy hours are rolling;
No sound save the requiem for the dead,
  Or knell of the death-bell tolling.

'Tis dead of night—not a sound is heard,
  Save from the night wind sighing;
Or the mournful moan of the midnight bird,
  To yon pale planet crying.

Who names the name of his murder'd child?
  What spears to the moon are glancing?
'Tis the vengeful cry of Shane Dymas wild,\*
  His bonnacht-men advancing.

Saw ye that cloud o'er the moonlight cast,
  Fire from its blackness breaking?
Heard ye that cry on the midnight blast,
  The voice of terror shrieking?

'Tis the fire from Ardsaillach's† willow'd height,
  Tower and temple falling;
'Tis the groan of death, and the cry of fright,
  From monks for mercy calling!

\* For an account of this fierce but high-souled chieftain, see Stuart's Historical Memoirs of the city of Armagh.
† "The Height of Willows," the ancient name of Armagh.

## THE LAST O'SULLIVAN BEARE.

### BY THOMAS D'ARCY M'GEE.

[Philip O'Sullivan Beare, a brave captain, and the author of many works relating to Ireland, commanded a ship-of-war for Philip IV. of Spain. In his "Catholic History," published at Lisbon in 1609, he has preserved the sad story of his family. It is in brief thus:—In 1602 his father's castle of Dunbuidhe, being demolished by cannonade, his family—consisting of a wife, son, and two daughters—emigrated to Spain, where his youngest brother, Donald, joined him professionally, but was soon after killed in an engagement with the Turks. The old chief, at the age of one hundred, died at Corunna, and was soon followed by his long-wedded wife. One daughter entered a convent and took the veil; the other, returning to Ireland, was lost at sea. In this version the real names have been preserved.]

ALL alone—all alone, where the gladsome vine is growing—
All alone by the bank of the Tagus darkly flowing,
No morning brings a hope for him, nor any evening cheer,
To O'Sullivan Beare thro' the seasons of the year.

He is thinking—ever thinking of the hour he left Dunbuidhe,
His father's staff fell from his hand, his mother wept wildly;
His brave young brother hid his face, his lovely sisters twain,
How they wrung their maiden hands to see him sail away for Spain.

They were Helen bright and Norah staid, who in their father's hall,
Like sun and shadow, frolicked round the grave armorial wall;
In Compostella's cloisters he found many a pictured saint,
But the Spirits boyhood canonised no human hand can paint.

All alone—all alone, where the gladsome vine is growing—
All alone by the bank of the Tagus darkly flowing—

No morning brings a hope for him, nor any evening
　　cheer,
To O'Sullivan Beare thro' the seasons of the year.

Oh! sure he ought to take a ship and sail back to Dun-
　　buidhe—
He ought to sail back, back again to that castle o'er the
　　sea;
His father, mother, brother, his lovely sisters twain,
'Tis they would raise the roof with joy to see him
　　back from Spain.

Hush! hush! I cannot tell it—the tale will make me
　　wild—
He left it, that grey castle, in age almost a child;
Seven long years with Saint James's Friars he conned
　　the page of might—
Seven long years for his father's roof was sighing every
　　night.

Then came a caravel from the north, deep freighted,
　　full of wo,
His houseless family it held, their castle it lay low,
Saint James's shrine, thro' ages famed as pilgrim haunt
　　of yore,
Saw never wanderers so wronged upon its scalloped
　　shore.

Yet it was sweet—their first grief past—to watch those
　　two fond girls
Sit by the sea, as mermaiden hold watch o'er hidden
　　pearls—
To see them sit and try to sing for that sire and mother
　　old
O'er whose heads five score winters their thickening
　　snows had rolled.

To hear them sing and pray in song for *them* in deadly
　　work,
Their gallant brothers battling for Spain against the
　　Turk—

Corunna's port at length they reach, and seaward ever
  stare,
Wondering what belates the ship their brothers home
  should bear.

Joy! joy!—it comes—their Philip lives!—ah! Donald
  is no more;
Like half a hope one son kneels down the exiled two before;
They spoke no requiem for the dead, nor blessing for the
  living;
The tearless heart of parentage has broken with its
  grieving.

Two pillars of a ruined pile—two old trees of the land—
Two voyagers on a sea of grief, long suff'rers hand in
  hand.
Thus at the woful tidings told left life and all its tears,
So died the wife of many a spring, the chief of an hun-
  dred years.

One sister is a black veiled nun of Saint Ursula, in
  Spain,
And one sleeps coldly far beneath the troubled Irish
  main;
Tis Helen bright who ventured to the arms of her true
  lover,
But Cleena's\* stormy waves now roll the radiant girl
  over.

All alone—all alone, where the gladsome vine is grow-
  ing—
All alone by the bank of the Tagus darkly flowing,
No morning brings a hope for him, nor any evening
  cheer,
To O'Sullivan Beare thro' the seasons of the year.

\* The waves off the coast of Cork, so called.

## THE ROBBER OF FERNEY.

The robber in his rocky hold from dawn of morning lay,
And wearily and drearily the noontide passed away—
The sun went down, and darkness fell in silence on the earth;
And now from out their wild retreat the robber band came forth.

That night by many a castle old, and many a haunted glen,
Mac Mahon and his outlaws rode, all wild and ruthless men;
Before them Lath-an-albany in midnight beauty lay—
Ah! woe is me! from all its fields the robber swept his prey.

And thus the country far and near, Mac Mahon held in awe,
And through this ancient barony, the robber's word was law;
In castle hall it chilled the sound of revelry and mirth,
But it lighted up with gladness still the lonely widow's hearth.

The robber bold, within his hold, from dawn of morning lies,
And gazes on the sinking sun with weary heart and eyes;
Till through the dark and starless night, by tower and ruin gray,
And far from all his faithful band he held his lonely way.

Alone among his enemies the outlawed chieftain stood,
With haughty eye, and fearless heart, and broadsword keen and good;
But his wild career is over, the castles of the land
Henceforth will need nor watch nor ward against the outlaw's band.

And now upon his homeward track, with heavy heart he
    goes—
No more in wild and midnight raid to burst upon his
    foes;
No more to lead his faithful band through Ferney's val-
    leys old,
No more within his mountain lair, carousal brave to
    hold.

Alas! alas! the light that guides both horse and rider on,
From many a kindling roof-tree burst, and many a dy-
    ing groan;
And many an agonizing shriek rings through the lurid
    air,
Oh! fearful is the carnage wrought within the robber's
    lair.

There's silence in the castle where the last Mac Mahon
    lies,
His heart is dull, the light of life has faded from his
    eyes;
But who can tell what dreams of woe—what visions of
    the dead—
What fond and broken-hearted forms surround the out
    law's bed?

Or who can tell what influence such blessed dreams
    impart,
Or why they still come thronging round the dying sin-
    ner's heart?—
Whate'er they be, the simple faith is rational and good
They come in that last hour to lead the wandering soul,
    to God.

## O'DONOGHUE'S BRIDE.

A MAIDEN dwelt, old legends say,
  Beside Loch Lene's mysterious waters,
And eye more bright, and heart more gay,
  Ne'er boasted earth's most gifted daughters

But shadows o'er her spirit came,
  Vague fancies fed the mind within;
And love sprung up with fatal flame,
  Where all things pure and good had been.

Alas! 'twere painful sight to see
  Upon the shore of that sweet lake,
The maiden gazing wistfully
  Upon the billows as they break.

So clearly pure, and purely bright,
  The first May-morn before her eyes,
With strange wild looks of love and light
  Waiting until her chief would rise.

Up from the waves he comes to her,
  O'Donoghue the brave, the gay,
So soon to be her worshipper,
  And bear her as his bride away.

Why comes he not? ah! can he prove
  Faithless? or does the maid but rave!
What could inspire this mystic love?—
  She springs into the yielding wave.

Down to the palace, deep beneath
  The clear blue lake, the maid is gone,
And the princely chief with a golden wreath
  Will place his bride on a royal throne.

## THE VIRGIN MARY'S BANK.

### BY J. J. CALLANAN.

[From the foot of Inchidony Island, an elevated tract of sand runs out into the sea, and terminates in a high green bank, which forms a pleasing contrast with the little desert behind it, and the black solitary rock immediately under. Tradition tells that the Virgin came one night to this hillock to pray, and was discovered kneeling there by the crew of a vessel that was coming to anchor near the place. They laughed at her piety, and made some merry and unbecoming remarks on her beauty, upon which a storm arose and destroyed the ship and her crew. Since that time no vessel has been known to anchor near the spot.]

The evening star rose beauteous above the fading day,
As to the lone and silent beach the Virgin came to pray,
And hill and wave shone brightly in the moonlight's mellow fall;
But the bank of green where Mary knelt was brightest of them all.

Slow moving o'er the waters, a gallant bark appear'd,
And her joyous crew look'd from the deck as to the land she near'd;
To the calm and shelter'd haven she floated like a swan,
And her wings of snow o'er the waves below in pride and beauty shone.

The master saw our Lady as he stood upon the prow,
And mark'd the whiteness of her robe and the radiance of her brow;
Her arms were folded gracefully upon her stainless breast,
And her eyes look'd up among the stars to Him her soul lov'd best.

He show'd her to his sailors, and he hail'd her with a cheer,
And on the kneeling Virgin they gazed with laugh and jeer;

And madly swore, a form so fair they never saw before;
And they curs'd the faint and lagging breeze that kept
　　them from the shore.

The ocean from its bosom shook off the moonlight
　　sheen,
And up its wrathful billows rose to vindicate their
　　Queen;
And a cloud came o'er the heavens, and a darkness o'er
　　the land,
And the scoffing crew beheld no more that Lady on the
　　strand.

Out burst the pealing thunder, and the light'ning leap'd
　　about;
And rushing with his watery war, the tempest gave a
　　shout;
And that vessel from a mountain wave came down with
　　thund'ring shock;
And her timbers flew like scatter'd spray on Inchidony's
　　rock.

Then loud from all that guilty crew one shriek rose wild
　　and high;
But the angry surge swept over them, and hush'd their
　　gurgling cry;
And with a hoarse exulting tone the tempest pass'd
　　away,
And down, still chafing from their strife, th' indignant
　　waters lay.

When the calm and purple morning shone out on high
　　Dunmore,
Full many a mangled corpse was seen on Inchidony's
　　shore;
And to this day the fisherman shows where the scoffers
　　sank:
And still he calls that hillock green, "the Virgin Mary's
　　bank."

# BALLADS OF THE AFFECTIONS.

## THE PARTING FROM SLEMISH; OR, THE CON'S FLIGHT TO TYRONE.

### BY SAMUEL FERGUSON, M.R.I.A.

[In Blackwood's Magazine, vol 34, there is a long and interesting story by Mr. Ferguson, entitled *The Return of Claneboy*. The events in the narrative are placed in the summer of 1333; and the hero of the tale is O'Neill, "the youngest of the Princes of Claneboy." The scene is laid, principally, in the county Antrim; and this ballad is supposed to have been sung in the tent of O'Neill, on Slemish, near Ballymena, on the first night after he had crossed the Bann, the boundary of the British Pale. The person supposed to sing is "Turlough," the Prince's harper.]

My Owen Bawn's hair is of thread of gold spun;
Of gold in the shadow, of light in the sun;
All curled in a coolun the bright tresses are—
They make his head radiant with beams like a star!

My Owen Bawn's mantle is long and is wide,
To wrap me up safe from the storm by his side;
And I'd rather face snow-drift and winter-wind there,
Than lie among daisies and sunshine elsewhere.

My Owen Bawn Con is a hunter of deer,
He tracks the dun quarry with arrow and spear—
Where wild woods are waving, and deep waters flow,
Ah, there goes my love, with the dun-dappled roe.

My Owen Bawn Con is a bold fisherman,
He spears the strong salmon in midst of the Bann;
And rock'd in the tempest on stormy Lough Neagh,
Draws up the red trout through the bursting of spray.

My Owen Bawn Con is a bard of the best,
He wakes me with singing, he sings me to rest;
And the cruit 'neath his fingers rings up with a sound,
As though angels harp'd o'er us, and fays underground.

They tell me the stranger has given command,
That crommeal and coolun shall cease in the land,
That all our youth's tresses of yellow be shorn,
And bonnets, instead, of a new fashion, worn;

That mantles like Owen Bawn's shield us no more,
That hunting and fishing henceforth we give o'er,
That the net and the arrow aside must be laid,
For hammer and trowel, and mattock and spade;

That the echoes of music must sleep in their caves,
That the slave must forget his own tongue for a slave's,
That the sounds of our lips must be strange in our ears,
And our bleeding hands toil in the dew of our tears.

Oh sweetheart and comfort! with thee by my side,
I could love and live happy, whatever betide;
But *thou*, in such bondage, wouldst die ere a day—
Away to Tir-oën, then, Owen, away!

There are wild woods and mountains, and streams deep
 and clear,
There are loughs in Tir-oën as lovely as here;
There are silver harps ringing in Yellow Hugh's hall,
And a bower by the forest side, sweetest of all!

We will dwell by the sunshiny skirts of the brake,
Where the sycamore shadows glow deep in the lake;
And the snowy swan stirring the green shadows there,
Afloat on the water, seems floating in air.

Farewell, then, black Slemish, green Collon adieu,
My heart is a-breaking at thinking of you;
But tarry we dare not, when freedom hath gone—
Away to Tir-oën, then, Owen Bawn Con!

Away to Tir-oën, then, Owen away!
We will leave them the dust from our feet for a prey,
And our dwelling in ashes and flames for a spoil—
'Twill be long ere they quench them with streams of
    the Foyle!

---

## AILLEEN.

#### BY JOHN BANIM.

'Tis not for love of gold I go,
  'Tis not for love of fame;
Tho' fortune should her smile bestow,
  And I may win a name,
            Ailleen,
  And I may win a name.

And yet it is for gold I go,
  And yet it is for fame,
That they may deck another brow,
  And bless another name,
            Ailleen,
  And bless another name.

For this, but this, I go—for this
  I lose thy love awhile;
And all the soft and quiet bliss
  Of thy young, faithful smile,
            Ailleen,
  Of thy young, faithful smile.

And I go to brave a world I hate,
  And woo it o'er and o'er,
And tempt a wave, and try a fate
  Upon a stranger shore,
                Ailleen,
  Upon a stranger shore.

Oh! when the bays are all my own,
  I know a heart will care!
Oh! when the gold is wooed and won,
  I know a brow shall wear,
                Ailleen,
  I know a brow shall wear!

And when with both returned again,
  My native land to see,
I know a smile will meet me there,
  And a hand will welcome me,
                Ailleen,
  And a hand will welcome me!

---

## EMAN-AC-KNUCK TO EVA.*

### BY J. B. CLARKE.

On the white hawthorn's bloom, in purpling streak,
I see the fairy-ring of morning break,
On the green valley's brow she golden glows,
Kissing the crimson of the opening rose,—
Knits with her thousand smiles its damask dyes,
And laughs the season on our hearts and eyes.
Rise, Eva, rise! fair spirit of my breast,
In whom I live, forsake the down of rest;

* Eman-ac-Knuck, or Ned of the Hill, a celebrated minstrel freebooter, who has been made the hero of a romance by Mrs. Peck. This poem is addressed to his wife.

Lovelier than morn, carnationed in soft hues,
Sweeter than rifled roses in the dews
Of dawn divinely weeping—and more fair
Than the coy flowers fann'd by mountain air;
More modest than the morning's blushing smile.
Rise, Eva, rise! pride of our Western Isle—
The sky's blue beauties lose their sunny grace
Before the calm, soft splendours of thy face;
Thy breath is sweeter than the apple bloom,
When spring's musk'd spirit bathes it in perfume;
The rock's wild honey steeps thy rubied lip—
Rise, Eva, rise!—I long these sweets to sip.
The polish'd ringlets of thy jetty locks
Shame the black ravens on their sun-gilt rocks;
Thy neck can boast a whiter, lovelier glow,
Than the wild cygnet's silvery plume of snow.
And from thy bosom, the soft throne of bliss,
The witch of love, in all her blessedness,
Heaves all her spells, wings all her feather'd darts,
And dips her arrows in adoring hearts.
Rise, Eva, rise! the sun sheds his sweet ray,
Am'rous to kiss thee—rise, my love! we'll stray
Across the mountain,—on the blossomy heath,
The heath-bloom holds for thee its odorous breath;
From the tall crag, aspiring to the skies,
I'll pick for thee the strings of strawberries;
The yellow nuts, too, from the hazel tree—
Soul of my heart!—I'll strip to give to thee:
As thy red lips the berries shall be bright,
And the sweet nuts shall be as ripe and white
And milky as the love-begotten tide
That fills thy spotless bosom, my sweet bride!
Queen of the smile of joy! shall I not kiss
Thee in the moss-grown cot, bless'd bower of bliss—
Shall not thy rapturous lover clasp thy charms,
And fold his Eva in his longing arms—
Shall Inniscather's wood again attest
Thy beauties strain'd unto this burning breast?
Absent how long! Ah! when wilt thou return?
When shall this wither'd bosom cease to mourn?

Eva! why stay so long? why leave me lone,
In the deep valley, to the cold gray stone
Pouring my plaints? O come, divinest fair!
Chase from my breast the demon of despair.
The winds are witness to my deep distress,
Like the lone wanderer of the wilderness,
For thee I languish and for thee I sigh—
My Eva, come, or thy poor swain shall die!
And didst thou hear my melancholy lay?
And art thou coming, love? My Eva! say?
Thou daughter of a meek-eyed dame, thy face
Is lovelier than thy mother's, in soft grace.
O yes! thou comest, Eva! to my sight
An angel minister of heavenly light:—
The sons of frozen climes can never see
Summer's bright smile so glad as I see thee:
Thy steps to me are lovelier than the ray
That roses night's cheek with the blush of day.

---

## O'DONNELL AND THE FAIR FITZGERALD.

### BY CHARLES GAVAN DUFFY.

A fawn that flies with sudden spring,
A wild-bird fluttering on the wing,
A passing gleam of April sun,
She flashed upon me, and was gone!
No chance did that dear face restore,
Nor then—nor now—nor evermore.
But sure, I see her in my dreams,
With eyes where love's first dawning beams;
And tones, like Irish music, say—
"You ask to love me, and you may;"
And so I know she *will* be mine,
That rose of princely Geraldine.

A voice that thrills with modest doubt,
A tale of love can ill pour out;
But, oh! when love wore manly guise,
And warrior feats woke woman's sighs—
With Irish sword, on Irish soil,
I might have won that kingly spoil.
But then, perchance, the Desmond race
Had deemed to mate with mine disgrace;
For mine's that strain of native blood
That last the Norman lance withstood;
And still when mountain war was waged
Their *sparths* among the Normans raged
And burst through many a serried line
Of Lacy, Burke, and Geraldine.

And yet methinks in battle press,
My love, I could not love you less;
For, oh! 'twere sweet brave deeds to do
For our old, sainted land, and you!
To sweep a storm, through Barrensmore,
With Docwra's scattered ranks before.
Like chaff upon our northern blast;
Nor rest till Bann's broad waves are passed,
Till Inbhar sees our flashing line,
Till Darha's lordly towers are mine,
And backward borne, as seal and sign,
The fairest maid of Geraldine.

But, Holy Bride,* how sweeter still
A hunted chief on Faughart hill,
With all the raging Pale behind,
So sweet, so strange a foe to find!
Soft love to plant where terror sprung,
With honey speech of Irish tongue;
Again to dare Clan-Geralt's swords
For hope of some sweet, stolen words.

* St. Bride, or Brigid.

Till many a danger passed and gone,
My suit has sped, my Bride is won—
She's proud Clan-Connell's Queen, and mine
Young Geraldine, of Geraldine.

But sure that time is dead and gone
When worth alone such love had won,
For hearts are cold, and hands are bought,
And faith, and lore, and love are nought?
Ah, trust me, no! The pure and true
The genial past may still renew;
Still love as then; and still no less
Strong hearts shall snatch a brave success,
And to their end right onward go,
As Erna's tide to Assaroe.\*
Oh! Saints may strive for Martyr's crown,
And warriors watch by leagured town,
But poor is all their toil to mine,
Till won's my Bride—my Geraldine!

## An Chuil-Fhionn.†

### TRANSLATED FROM THE IRISH.

### BY SAMUEL FERGUSON, M.R.I.A.

Oh, had you seen the Coolun,
  Walking down by the cuckoo's street,‡
With the dew of the meadows shining
  On her milk-white twinkling feet.

---

\* A waterfall in Tyrconnell, the O'Donnell's county.
† The Coolun, the Maiden of fair flowing Locks.—See another ballad with this name, page 199.
‡ This word is incorrectly and unintelligibly printed in the original. I am helped, I believe, to the proper word by the following passage in Mr. Ferguson's first article on Hardiman's Minstrelsy (*University Magazine*, vol iii. 477.) "The bagpipes are drawing their last breath from a few consumptive lungs, and French horns have been heard in 'the street of the cuckoos.'"

Oh, my love she is, and my *coleen oge*,
   And she dwells in Bal'nagar;
And she bears the palm of beauty bright
   From the fairest that in Erin are.

In Bal'nagar is the Coolun,
   Like the berry on the bough her cheek;
Bright beauty dwells for ever
   On her fair neck and ringlets sleek:
Oh, sweeter is her mouth's soft music
   Than the lark or thrush at dawn,
Or the blackbird in the greenwood singing
   Farewell to the setting sun.

Rise up, my boy! make ready
   My horse, for I forth would ride,
To follow the modest damsel,
   Where she walks on the green hill side:
For e'er since our youth were we plighted,
   In faith, troth, and wedlock true—
Oh, she's sweeter to me nine times over,
   Than organ or cuckoo!

Oh, ever since my childhood
   I loved the fair and darling child,
But our people came between us,
   And with lucre our pure love defiled:
Oh, my wo it is, and my bitter pain,
   And I weep it night and day,
That the *coleen bawn* of my early love
   Is torn from my heart away.

Sweet-heart and faithful treasure,
   Be constant still, and true;
Nor for want of herds and houses
   Leave one who would ne'er leave you.
I'll pledge you the blessed Bible,
   Without and eke within,
That the faithful God will provide for us
   Without thanks to kith or kin.

Oh, love, do you remember
When we lay all night alone,
Beneath the ash in the winter-storm,
When the oak wood round did groan?
No shelter then from the blast had we,
The bitter blast or sleet,
But your gown to wrap about our heads
And my coat around our feet.

## Bpiȝidin Ban Mo Stop.*

### BY EDWARD WALSH.

[*Brighidin ban mo stor* is in English *fair young bride*, or *Bridget my treasure*. The proper sound of this phrase is not easily found by the mere English-speaking Irish. The following is the best help I can afford them in the case:—" *Bree-dheen-bawn-mu-sthore.*" The proper name Brighit, or Bride, signifies *a fiery dart*, and was the name of the goddess of poetry in the Pagan days of Ireland.]

I AM a wand'ring minstrel man,
And Love my only theme,
I've stray'd beside the pleasant Bann,
And eke the Shannon's stream;
I've pip'd and play'd to wife and maid
By Barrow, Suir, and Nore,
But never met a maiden yet
Like Bpiȝidin Ban Mo Stop.

My girl hath ringlets rich and rare,
By Nature's fingers wove—
Loch-Carra's swan is not so fair
As is her breast of love;
And when she moves, in Sunday sheen,
Beyond our cottage door,
I'd scorn the high-born Saxon queen
For Bpiȝidin Ban Mo Stop.

* Brighidin Ban Mo Store.

It is not that thy smile is sweet,
  And soft thy voice of song—
It is not that thou fleest to meet
  My comings lone and long;
But that doth rest beneath thy breast,
  A heart of purest core,
Whose pulse is known to me alone,
  Mo Bṙıᵹıṅ Baṅ aṙṫoṅ.

---

## THE LAMENTATION OF FELIX M‘CARTHY.

### TRANSLATED FROM THE IRISH.

### BY J. J. CALLANAN.

[From the inquiries we have made (says the author) concerning the tragical circumstance that gave rise to the following effusion, we learn that Felix M‘Carthy had been compelled, during a period of disturbance and persecution, to fly for safety to a mountainous region in the western part of this county (Cork). He was accompanied in his flight by a wife and four children, and found an asylum in a lone and secluded glen, where he constructed a rude kind of habitation, as a temporary residence. One night, during the absence of himself and his wife, this ill-contrived structure suddenly gave way, and buried the four children, who were asleep at the time, in its ruins. What the feelings of the father were will be best learned from the following lamentation.]

I'LL sing my children's death song, tho'
My voice is faint and low;
Mine is the heart that's desolate—
'Tis I will mourn their fate.

I'll sing their death song, tho' the dart
Is rankling in my heart:
No friend is here my pangs to soothe,
In this deep solitude.

Weep not the widow's grief to see,
When wild with agony!
Nor mourn to hear the bridegroom rave,
Above his partner's grave.

But weep for one whose bitter wail,
Is poured upon the gale,
Like the shrill bird that flutters nigh
The nest, where its crushed offspring lie.

Yes! I will sing this song of wo,
Till life's last spark shall glow.
Like the swan floating on the surge,
That murmurs its unwilling dirge.

Thou Callaghan, devoid of sin—
And Charles of the silken skin,
Mary and Anne, my peerless flower,
Entombed within an hour.

My four sweet children fair and brave,
Laid in one grave—
Wound of my soul, that I should say
Your death song in one day!

Vain was the blood of Eiver's race,
And every opening grace,
And youth undarkened by a cloud—
Against an early shroud!

Mute are the tongues that sung for me,
In joyful harmony:—
Cold are the lips whose welcome kiss
To me was heavenly bliss.

Oh! but for him whose head was bow'd
'Mid Calvary's mocking crowd—
Soon would I fly the painful day,
And follow in their way.

Yet mourned not He in voiceless gloom,
O'er Lazarus in the tomb—
Rushed not the flood from his dimm'd eyes?
Heav'd not his breast with sighs?

Yes, for *his kindred* from the day,
That earthward darkling lay,—
Then do not chide that I should mourn
For them that *won't return.*

And mourned not the pure Virgin, when
Her Son, transfixed by men,
Writh'd in the throes of his dark agony?
Then blame not me.

At midnight's hour of silence deep,
Seal'd in their balmy sleep,
Oh! crushing grief,—oh! scathing blow,
My lov'd ones were laid low.

Methought, when bow'd this head with time,
Around me they would twine,
Nor reck'd that I should mourn their lot,
A thing of nought.

'Twas meet to him, affection they should prove
Who gave them all his love,
And to old age the night concede,
Their path to lead.

Beauty and strength have left my brow,
Nor care nor wisdom have I now;
Little the blow of death I dread
Since all my hopes have fled.

No more—no more shall music's voice,
My heart rejoice—
Like a brain-stricken fool, whose ear
Is clos'd 'gainst earthly cheer,

When wailing at the dead of night,
They cross my aching sight—
They come, and beck'ning me away,
They chide my long delay.

At midnight hour—at morn—at eve,
My sight they do not leave;
Within—abroad—their looks of love,
Around me move.

Oh! in their visits no affection's lost!
I love the pathways by their shadows cross'd,
Soon, by the will of heaven's King,
To their embrace I'll spring.

I pity her who never more will know
Contentment here below:
Who fed them at the fountain of her breast,
And hush'd their infant rest.

Her faded eyes, her anguish speak—
And her clasp'd hands, so weak!—
'Tis she, alas! of Erin's daughters
Hath seen* the *ruin of slaughters.*†

---

## PASTHEEN FION.

#### TRANSLATED FROM THE IRISH.

#### BY SAMUEL FERGUSON, M.R.I.A.

[In Hardiman's "Irish Minstrelsy," vol. 1, p. 330, there is a note upon the original of *Paistheen Fion.* The name may be translated either fair youth or fair maiden, and the writer supposes it to have a political meaning, and to refer to the son of James II. Whatever may have been the intention of the author, it is, on the surface, an exquisite love song, and as such I have retained it in this class of ballads, rather than in the next.—ED.]

OH, my fair Pastheen is my heart's delight;
Her gay heart laughs in her blue eye bright;

---

\* This last expression may appear strange to the English reader, but it is a literal translation of the original.—AUTHOR'S NOTE.

† This poem is taken from "Bolster's Quarterly Magazine," vol. 1, Cork, 1826. It is not included in the collection of Callanan's Poems, published in 1829, in London.—"Cusheen Loo," p. 78, is also taken from the same magazine, and is likewise omitted from the collection.

Like the apple blossom her bosom white,
And her neck like the swan's on a March morn bright!
 Then, Oro, come with me! come with me! come
  with me!
 Oro, come with me! brown girl, sweet!
 And, oh! I would go through snow and sleet
 If you would come with me, my brown girl, sweet!

Love of my heart, my fair Pastheen!
Her cheeks are as red as the rose's sheen,
But my lips have tasted no more, I ween,
Than the glass I drank to the health of my queen!
 Then, Oro, come with me! come with me! come
  with me!
 Oro, come with me! brown girl, sweet!
 And, oh! I would go through snow and sleet
 If you would come with me, my brown girl, sweet!

Were I in the town, where's mirth and glee,
Or 'twixt two barrels of barley bree,
With my fair Pastheen upon my knee,
'Tis I would drink to her pleasantly!
 Then, Oro, come with me! come with me! come
  with me!
 Oro, come with me! brown girl, sweet!
 And, oh! I would go through snow and sleet
 If you would come with me, my brown girl, sweet!

Nine nights I lay in longing and pain,
Betwixt two bushes, beneath the rain,
Thinking to see you, love, once again;
But whistle and call were all in vain!
 Then, Oro, come with me! come with me! come
  with me!
 Oro, come with me! brown girl, sweet!
 And, oh! I would go through snow and sleet
 If you would come with me, my brown girl, sweet!

I'll leave my people, both friend and foe;
From all the girls in the world I'll go;

But from you, sweetheart, oh, never! oh, no!
'Till I lie in the coffin stretched, cold and low!
   Then, Oro, come with me! come with me! come
      with me!
   Oro, come with me! brown girl, sweet!
   And, oh! I would go through snow and sleet
    If you would come with me, my brown girl, sweet!

## THE PATRIOT'S BRIDE.

### BY CHARLES GAVAN DUFFY.

Oh! give me back that royal dream
    My fancy wrought,
When I have seen your sunny eyes
    Grow moist with thought;
And fondly hop'd, dear Love, your heart from mine
    Its spell had caught;
And laid me down to dream that dream divine,
    But true methought,
Of how *my* life's long task would be, to make *yours*
    blessed as it ought.

To learn to love sweet Nature more
    For your sweet sake,
To watch with you—dear friend, with you!—
    Its wonders break;
To see the sparkling spring in that bright face
    Its mirror make—
On summer morns to hear the sweet birds sing
    By linn and lake;
And know your voice, your magic voice, could still a
    grander music wake!

On some old shell-strewn rock to sit
    In autumn eves,
Where gray Killiney cools the torrid air
    Hot autumn weaves;

Or by that Holy Well in mountain lone,
      Where Faith believes
(Fain would I b'lieve) its secret, darling, wish
      The heart achieves.
Yet, oh, its Saint was not more pure than she to whom
      my fond heart cleaves.

To see the dank mid-winter night
      Pass like a noon,
Heated with thought from minds that teemed,
      And glowed like June:
Where Art would pass in sculp'd and pictured train
      Its magic boon;
And Music thrill with many a haughty strain,
      And dear old tune,
Till hearts grew sad to hear the destined hour to part
      had come so soon.

To wake the old weird world that sleeps
      In Irish lore;
The strains sweet foreign Spenser sung
      By Mulla's shore;
Dear Curran's airy thoughts, like purple birds
      That shine and soar;
Tone's fiery hopes, and Grattan's thunder-words
      A nation swore;
The songs that once our own dear Davis sung; ah, me!
      to sing no more.

To search with mother-love the gifts
      Our land can boast—
Soft Erna's isles, Neagh's wooded copes,
      Clare's iron coast;
Kildare, whose legends gray our bosoms stir
      With fay and ghost;
Gray Mourne, green Antrim, purple Glenmalur—
      Lene's fairy host;
With raids to many a foreign land to learn to love dear
      Ireland most.

And all those proud old victor-fields
    We thrill to name;
Whose mem'ries are the stars that light
    Long nights of shame;
The Cairn, the Dun, the Rath, the Tower, the Keep,
    That still proclaim
In chronicles of clay and stone, how true, how deep,
    Was Eirè's fame,
Oh! we shall see them all, with her, that dear, dear
    friend we two have loved the same.

Yet ah! how truer, tend'rer still
    Methought did seem
That scene of tranquil joy, that happy home,
    By Dodder's stream;
The morning smile, that grew a fixèd star
    With love-lit beam,
The ringing laugh, locked hands, and all the far
    And shining stream
Of daily love, that made our daily life diviner than a
    dream.

For still to me dear friend, dear Love,
    Or both—dear Wife,
Your image comes with serious thoughts,
    But tender, rife;
No petted plaything to caress or chide
    In sport or strife;
But my best chosen friend, companion, guide,
    To walk through life
Link'd hand in hand, two equal, loving friends, true
    husband and true wife.

## COULIN.

### BY CAROLL MALONE.

[In the twenty-eighth year of the reign of Henry VIII. an act was made respecting the habits and dress in general of the Irish, whereby all persons were restrained from being shorn or shaven above the ears, or from wearing glibbes, or Coulins (long locks) on their heads, or hair on their upper lip, called Crommeal. On this occasion a song was written by one of our bards, in which an Irish virgin is made to give the preference to her dear Coulin (or the youth with the flowing locks), to all strangers (by which the English were meant), or those who wore their habits. Of this song the air alone has reached us, and is universally admired.—*Walker, as quoted in Moore's Melodies.*

It so happens, however, on turning to the above statute, that no mention is to be found therein of the Coulin. But in the year 1295, a Parliament was held in Dublin; and then an act was passed which more than expressly names the Coulin, and minutely describes it for its more effectual prohibition. This, the only statute made in Ireland that names the Coulin, was passed two hundred and forty-two years before the act cited by Mr. Moore; and, in consequence of it, some of the Irish Chieftains who lived near the seat of English government, or wished to keep up intercourse with the English districts, did, in or soon after that year, 1295, cut off their Coulins, and a distinct memorial of the event was made in writing by the Officers of the Crown. It was on this occasion that the bard, ever adhesive to national habits, endeavoured to fire the patriotism of a conforming chieftain; and, in the character of some favourite virgin, declares her preference for her lover with the Coulin, before him who complaisantly assumed the adornments of foreign fashion.—*Dublin Penny Journal.*]

The last time she looked in the face of her dear,
She breathed not a sigh, and she shed not a tear;
But she took up his harp, and she kissed his cold cheek—
" 'Tis the first, and the last, for thy Norah to seek."

For beauty and bravery Cathan was known,
And the long flowing coulin he wore in Tyrone;
The sweetest of singers and harpers was he,
All over the North, from the Bann to the sea.

O'er the marshes of Dublin he often would rove,
To the glens of O'Toole, where he met with his love;
And at parting they pledged that, next midsummer's day,
He would come for the last time, and bear her away.

The king had forbidden the men of O'Neal,
With the coulin adorned, to come o'er the pale;
But Norah was Irish, and said, in her pride,
"If he wear not his coulin, I'll ne'er be his bride."

The bride has grown pale as the robe that she wears,
For the Lammas is come, and no bridegroom appears;
And she hearkens and gazes, when all are at rest,
For the sound of his harp and the sheen of his vest.

Her palfrey is pillioned, and she has gone forth
On the long rugged road that leads down to the North;—
Where Eblana's strong castle frowns darkly and drear,
Is the head of her Cathan upraised on a spear.

The Lords of the Castle had murdered him there,
And all for the wearing that poor lock of hair:
For the word she had spoken in mirth or in pride,
Her lover, too fond and too faithful, had died.

'Twas then that she looked in the face of her dear,
She breathed not a sigh, and she dropped not a tear;
She took up his harp, and she kissed his cold cheek:
"Farewell! 'tis the first for thy Norah to seek."

And afterward, oft would the wilderness ring,
As, at night, in sad strains, to that harp she would
    sing
Her heartbreaking tones,—we remember them well,
But the words of her wailing, no mortal can tell.

## MAURYEEN.

THE cottage is here as of old I remember,
    The pathway is worn as it always hath been;
On the turf-piled hearth there still lives a bright ember,
    But where is Mauryeen?

The same pleasant prospect still lieth before me,—
    The river—the mountain—the valley of green;
And heaven itself (a bright blessing!) is o'er me:—
    But where is Mauryeen?

Lost! lost! like a dream that hath come and departed
    (Ah, why are the loved and the lost ever seen?)
She has fallen—hath flown—with a lover false-hearted—
    So mourn for Mauryeen!

And she who so loved her is slain—(the poor mother!)
    Struck dead in a day by a shadow unseen;
And the home we once loved is the home of another—
    And lost is Mauryeen!

Sweet Shannon, a moment by thee let me ponder—
    A moment look back to the things that have been:
Then away to the world, where the ruin'd ones wander,
    To seek for Mauryeen!

Pale peasant, perhaps, 'neath the frown of high Heaven,
    She roams the dark deserts of sorrow unseen,
Unpitied—unknown; but I—*I* shall know even
    The *ghost* of Mauryeen!

## A LAMENT.

### BY D. F. M'CARTHY.

*Ya esta llama se desata,*
*Ya caduca este edificio,*
*Ya se desmaya esta flor.*

The dream is over,
The vision has flown;
Dead leaves are lying
Where roses have blown;
Wither'd and strown
Are the hopes I cherished,
All have perished
But grief alone.

My heart was a garden
Where fresh leaves grew;
Flowers there were many,
And weeds a few;
Cold winds blew,
And the frosts came thither,
For flowers will wither,
And weeds renew!

Youth's bright palace
Is overthrown,
With its diamond sceptre
And golden throne;
As a time-worn stone
Its turrets are humbled,
All have crumbled
But grief alone!

Whither, oh! whither
Have fled away
The dreams and hopes
Of my early day?

Ruined and gray
Are the towers I builded;
And the beams that gilded—
Ah! where are they?

Once this world
Was fresh and bright,
With its golden noon
And its starry night;
Glad and light,
By mountain and river,
Have I bless'd the Giver
With hushed delight.

These were the days
Of story and song,
When Hope had a meaning
And Faith was strong.
"Life will be long,
And lit with Love's gleamings;"
Such were my dreamings,
But, ah! how wrong!

Youth's illusions,
One by one,
Have passed like clouds
That the sun looked on.
While morning shone,
How purple their fringes!
How ashy their tinges
When that was gone!

Darkness that cometh
Ere morn has fled—
Boughs that wither
Ere fruits are shed—
Death bells instead
Of a bridal's pealings—
Such are my feelings,
Since Hope is dead!

Sad is the knowledge
That cometh with years—
Bitter the tree
That is watered with tears;
Truth appears,
With his wise predictions,
Then vanish the fictions
Of boyhood's years.

As fire-flies fade
When the nights are damp,
As meteors are quenched
In a stagnant swamp—
Thus Charlemagne's camp
Where the Paladins rally,
And the Diamond Valley
And Wonderful Lamp,

And all the wonders
Of Ganges and Nile,
And Haroun's rambles,
And Crusoe's isle,
And Princes who smile
On the Genii's daughters,
'Neath the Orient waters
Full many a mile.

And all that the pen
Of Fancy can write,
Must vanish
In manhood's misty light,
Squire and knight,
And damosel's glances,
Sunny romances
So pure and bright!

These have vanished,
And what remains?
Life's budding garlands
Have turned to chains—

Its beams and rains
Feed but docks and thistles—
And sorrow whistles
O'er desert plains!

The dove will fly
From a ruined nest—
Love will not dwell
In a troubled breast—
The heart has no zest
To sweeten life's dolor—
If Love, the Consoler,
Be not its guest!

The dream is over,
The vision has flown;
Dead leaves are lying
Where roses have blown;
Wither'd and strown
Are the hopes I cherished,
All have perished
But grief alone!

## YOUNG KATE OF KILCUMMER.

[Kilcnmmer is in the County of Cork, on the east side of the river Awbeg, not far distant from the town of Doneraile.]

THERE are flowers in the valley,
   And fruit on the hill,
Sweet-scented and smiling,
   Resort where you will.
But the sweetest and brightest,
   In spring-time or summer,
Is the girl of my heart,
   The young Kate of Kilcummer.

Oh! I'd wander from day-break
   Till night's gloomy fall,
Full sure such another
   I'd ne'er meet at all.

As the rose to the bee,
　As the sunshine to summer,
So welcome to me
　Is young Kate of Kilcummer.

---

## THE MOUNTAIN DEW.

### BY SAMUEL LOVER.

By yon mountain tipp'd with cloud,
By the torrent foaming loud,
By the dingle where the purple bells of heather grew,
Where the Alpine flow'rs are hid,
And where bounds the nimble kid,
There we wandered both together through the mountain dew!
With what delight in summer's night we trod the twilight gloom,
The air so full of fragrance from the flowers so full of bloom,
And our hearts so full of joy—for aught else there was no room,
And we wandered both together through the mountain dew.

Those sparkling gems that rest
On the mountain's flow'ry breast
Are like the joys we number—they are light and few.
For a while to earth are given,
And are called again to heaven,
When the spirit of the morning steals the mountain dew.
But memory, angelic, makes a heaven on earth for men,
Her rosy light recalleth bright the dew-drops back again,
The warmth of love exhales them from that well-remembered glen,
Where we wandered both together through the tain dew!

# POLITICAL BALLADS.

## THE MUSTER OF THE NORTH.

### A.D. 1641.

#### BY CHARLES GAVAN DUFFY.

[We deny, and have always denied, the alleged massacre of 1641. But that the people rose under their Chiefs, seized the English towns, and expelled the English settlers, and in doing so committed many excesses, is undeniable—as is equally the desperate provocation. The Ballad here printed is not meant as an apology for these excesses, which we condemn and lament, but as a true representation of the feelings of the insurgents in the first madness of success.]

Joy! joy! the day is come at last, the day of hope and pride,
And see! our crackling bonfires light old Banna's joyful tide,
And gladsome bell, and bugle horn, from Inbhar's* captured Towers,
Hark! how they tell the Saxon swine, this land is ours, IS OURS!

Glory to God! my eyes have seen the ransomed fields of Down,
My ears have drunk the joyful news, "Stout Feidhlim† hath his own."
Oh! may they see and hear no more, oh! may they rot to clay,
When they forget to triumph in the conquest of to-day.

\* Newry.  † Phelim.

Now, now we'll teach the shameless Scot to purge his
    thievish maw,
Now, now the courts may fall to pray, for justice is the law,
Now shall the Undertaker* square for once his loose
    accounts,
We ll strike, brave boys, a fair result, from all his false
    amounts.

Con e, trample down their robber rule, and smite its
    venal spawn,
Their foreign laws, their foreign church, their ermine
    and their lawn,
With all the specious fry of fraud that robb'd us of our
    own;
And plant our ancient laws again, beneath our lineal
    throne.

Ou standard flies o'er fifty towers, o'er twice ten thou-
    sand men;
Dc n have we pluck'd the pirate Red, never to rise
    agen;
The Green alone shall stream above our native field and
    flood—
The spotless Green, save where its folds are gemmed
    with Saxon blood!

Pity!† no, no; you dare not, Priest—not you, our Fa-
    ther, dare
Preach to us now that Godless creed—the murderer's
    blood to spare;
To spare his blood, while tombless still our slaughtered
    kin implore
" Graves and revenge" from Gobbin-Cliffs and Carrick's
    bloody shore ! ‡

* The Scotch and English adventurers planted in Ulster by James I
were called Undertakers.
† Leland, the Protestant Historian, states that the Catholic Priests
"laboured zealously to moderate the excesses of war;" and frequently pro-
tected the English by concealing them in their places of worship, and
even under their altars.
‡ The scene of the dreadful massacre of the unoffending inhabitants
of Island Magee, by the garrison of Carrickfergus

Pity !—could we "forget—forgive," if we were clods of clay,
Our martyred priests, our banished chiefs, our race in dark decay,
And worse than all—you know it, Priest—the daughters of our land,
With wrongs we blushed to name until the sword was in our hand!

Pity ! well, if you needs must whine, let pity have its way,
Pity for all our comrades true, far from our side to-day;
The prison-bound who rot in chains, the faithful dead who poured
Their blood 'neath Temple's lawless axe or Parsons' ruffian sword.

They smote us with the swearer's oath, and with the murderer's knife,
We in the open field will fight, fairly for land and life;
But, by the Dead and all their wrongs, and by our hopes to-day,
One of us twain shall fight their last, or be it we or they—

They banned our faith, they banned our lives, they trod us into earth,
Until our very patience stirred their bitter hearts to mirth;
Even this great flame that wraps them now, not *we* but *they* have bred,
Yes, this is their own work, and now, their work be on their head.

Nay, Father, tell us not of help from Leinster's Norman Peers,
If that we shape our holy cause to match their selfish fears—

Helpless and hopeless be their cause, who brook a vain
 delay,
Our ship is launched, our flag's afloat, whether they
 come or stay.
Let silken Howth, and savage Slane still kiss their
 tyrant's rod,
And pale Dunsany still prefer his Master to his God;
Little we heed their father's sons the Marchmen of the
 Pale,
If Irish hearts and Irish hands have Spanish blades
 and mail?

Then, let them stay to bow and fawn, or fight with cunning words;
I fear me more their courtly arts than England's hire-
 ling swords;
Natheless their creed they hate us still, as the Despoiler
 hates,
Could they love us and love their prey—our kinsmen's lost estates!

Our rude array's a jagged rock to smash the spoiler's
 power,
Or need we aid, His aid we have who doomed this gracious hour;
Of yore He led his Hebrew host to peace through strife
 and pain,
And us He leads the self-same path, the self-same goal
 to gain.

Down from the sacred hills whereon a SAINT* communed
 with God,
Up from the vale where Bagnall's blood manured the
 reeking sod,
Out from the stately woods of Triuch,† M'Kenna's plundered home,
Like Malin's waves, as fierce and fast, our faithful clansmen come.

 * St. Patrick, whose favourite retreat was Leath Chathail, (Lecale
Cathal's half,) in the county Down.
 † Improperly written Truagh.

Then, brethren, on !—O'Neill's dear shade would frown
 to see you pause—
Our banished Hugh, our martyred Hug
 o'er your cause—
His gen'rous error lost the land—he deem'd the Norman true,
Oh, forward! friends, it must not lose the land again in
 you!

---

## DARK ROSALEEN.

#### TRANSLATED FROM THE IRISH

### BY JAMES CLARENCE MANGAN.

[This impassioned ballad, entitled in the original *Roisin Duh* (or The Black Little Rose), was written in the reign of Elizabeth by one of the poets of the celebrated Tirconnellian chieftain, Hugh the Red O'Donnell. It purports to be an allegorical address from Hugh to Ireland on the subject of his love and struggles for her, and his resolve to raise her again to the glorious position she held as a nation before the irruption of the Saxon and Norman spoilers. The true character and meaning of the figurative allusions with which it abounds, and to two only of which I need refer here—viz., the "Roman wine" and "Spanish ale" mentioned in the first stanza—the intelligent reader will, of course, find no difficulty in understanding.]

O my Dark Rosaleen,
 Do not sigh, do not weep!
The priests are on the ocean green,
 They march along the deep.
There's wine...from the royal Pope,
 Upon the ocean green;
And Spanish ale shall give you hope,
 My Dark Rosaleen!
 My own Rosaleen!
Shall glad your heart, shall give you hope,
Shall give you health, and help, and hope,
 My Dark Rosaleen!

Over hills, and through dales,
  Have I roamed for your sake;
All yesterday I sailed with sails
  On river and on lake.
The Erne,...at its highest flood,
  I dashed across unseen,
For there was lightning in my blood,
  My Dark Rosaleen!
  My own Rosaleen!
Oh! there was lightning in my blood,
Red lightning lightened through my blood,
  My Dark Rosaleen!


All day long, in unrest,
  To and fro, do I move.
The very soul within my breast
  Is wasted for you, love!
The heart...in my bosom faints
  To think of you, my queen,
My life of life, my saint of saints,
  My Dark Rosaleen!
  My own Rosaleen!
To hear your sweet and sad complaints,
My life, my love, my saint of saints,
  My Dark Rosaleen!


Wo and pain, pain and wo,
  Are my lot, night and noon,
To see your bright face clouded so,
  Like to the mournful moon.
But yet......will I rear your throne
  Again in golden sheen;
'Tis you shall reign, shall reign alone,
  My Dark Rosaleen!
  My own Rosaleen!
'Tis you shall have the golden throne,
'Tis you shall reign, and reign alone,
  My Dark Rosaleen!

Over dews, over sands,
  Will I fly, for your weal:
Your holy delicate white hands
  Shall girdle me with steel.
At home......in your emerald bowers,
  From morning's dawn till e'en,
You'll pray for me, my flower of flowers,
  My Dark Rosaleen!
  My fond Rosaleen!
You'll think of me through daylight's hours,
My virgin flower, my flower of flowers,
  My Dark Rosaleen!

. could scale the blue air,
  I could plough the high hills,
Oh, I could kneel all night in prayer,
  To heal your many ills!
And one......beamy smile from you
  Would float like light between
My toils and me, my own, my true,
  My Dark Rosaleen!
  My fond Rosaleen!
Would give me life and soul anew,
A second life, a soul anew,
  My Dark Rosaleen!

O! the Erne shall run red
  With redundance of blood,
The earth shall rock beneath our tread,
  And flames wrap hill and wood,
And gun-peal, and slogan cry,
  Wake many a glen serene,
Ere you shall fade, ere you shall die,
  My Dark Rosaleen!
  My own Rosaleen!
The Judgment Hour must first be nigh,
Ere you can fade, ere you can die,
  My Dark Rosaleen!

## DRIMIN DHU.

#### A JACOBITE RELIC—TRANSLATED FROM THE IRISH.

#### BY SAMUEL FERGUSON, M.R.I.A.

Ah, Drimin Dhu deelish, a pride of the flow,*
Ah, where are your folks, are they living or no?
They're down in the ground, 'neath the sod lying low,
Expecting King James with the crown on his brow.

But if I could get sight of the crown on his brow,
By night and day travelling to London I'd go;
Over mountains of mist and soft mosses below,
Till I'd beat on the kettle-drums, Drimin Dhubh, O!

Welcome home, welcome home, Drimin Dhubh, O!
Good was your sweet milk, for drinking I trow;
With your face like a rose, and your dew-lap of snow,
I'll part from you never, ah, Drimin Dhubh, O!

## SHANE BWEE; OR, THE CAPTIVITY OF THE GAEL.

### Ɓeıbıoɲɲ ɲa-ɲ-Ɓaoıɒeıl.

#### BY JAMES CLARENCE MANGAN.

[A Translation of the Jacobite song called "Géiblonn na-n-Gaoideil," written by Owen Roe O'Sullivan, a Kerry poet, who flourished about the middle of the last century.†]

'Twas by sunset...I walked and wandered
  Over hill sides...and over moors,

---

\* The soft grassy part of the bog.
† His death, it has been stated by Mr. Edward Walshe—a gentleman, by the way, to whose literary exertions Ireland is indebted almost beyond her power of repayment—occurred in the year 1784. We may, therefore, suppose this song to have been written by the author in his youth—perhaps about the year 1740

With a many sighs and tears
Sunk in sadness,...I darkly pondered
All the wrongs our...lost land endures
In these latter night-black years.
"How," I mused, "has her worth departed!
What a ruin...her fame is now!
We, once free-est of the Free,
We are trampled...and broken-hearted·
Yea, even our Princes...themselves must bow
Low before the vile Shane Bwee!"\*

Nigh a stream, in...a grassy hollow,
Tired, at length, I...lay down to rest—
There the birds and balmy air
Bade new reveries...and cheerier follow,
Waking newly...within my breast
Thoughts that cheated my despair.
Was I waking...or was I dreaming?
I glanced up, and...behold! there shone
Such a vision over me!
A young girl, bright...as Erin's beaming
Guardian spirit—now sad and lone,
Through the Spoiling of Shane Bwee!

O, for pencil...to paint the golden
Locks that waved in...luxuriant sheen
To her feet of stilly light!
(Not the Fleece that...in ages olden
Jason bore o'er...the ocean green
Into Hellas, gleamed so bright.)
And the eyebrows...thin-arch'd over
Her mild eyes, and...more, even more
Beautiful, methought, to see
Than those rainbows...that wont to hover
O'er our blue island-lakes of yore,
Ere the Spoiling by Shane Bwee!

---

\* *Seagan Buidhe*, Yellow John, a name applied first to the Prince of Orange, and afterwards to his adherents generally.

"Bard!" she spake, "deem...not this unreal
I was niece of...a Pair whose peers
  None shall see on Earth agen—
Æongus Con, and...the Dark O'Niall,
  Rulers over...Iern in years
    When her sons as yet were Men.
Times have darkened;...and now our holy
  Altars crumble,...and castles fall;
    Our groans ring through Christendee.
Still, despond not! HE comes, though slowly,
  He, the Man, who shall disenthral
    The PROUD CAPTIVE of Shane Bwee!"

Here she vanished;...and I, in sorrow
  Blent with joy, rose...and went my way
    Homeward over moor and hill.
O, Great God! Thou...from whom we borrow
  Life and strength, unto Thee I pray!
    Thou, who swayest at Thy will
Hearts and councils,...thralls, tyrants, freemen,
  Wake through Europe...the ancient soul,
    And on every shore and sea,
From the Blackwater to the Dniemen,
  Freedom's Bell will...ere long time toll
    The deep death-knell of Shane Bwee!

---

## THE VOICE OF LABOUR.

### A CHANT OF THE CITY MEETINGS.

### A. D. 1843.

### BY CHARLES GAVAN DUFFY.

YE who despoil the sons of toil, saw ye this sight to-day,
When stalwart trade in long brigade, beyond a king's array

\* Niall Dubh.

Marched in the blessed light of heaven, beneath the
 open sky,
Strong in the might of sacred RIGHT, that none dare
 ask them why?
These are the slaves, the needy knaves, ye spit upon
 with scorn—
The spawn of earth, of nameless birth, and basely bred
 as born;
Yet know, ye weak and silken lords, were we the thing
 ye say,
Your broad domains, your coffered gains, your lives were
 ours to-day!

Measure that rank, from flank to flank; 'tis fifty thousand strong;
And mark you here, in front and rear, brigades as deep
 and long;
And know that never blade of foe, or Arran's deadly
 breeze,
Tried by assay of storm or fray, more dauntless hearts
 than these;
The sinewy Smith, little he recks of his own child—the
 sword;
The men of gear, think you they fear *their* handiwork
 —a Lord?
And undismayed, yon sons of trade might see the battle's front,
Who bravely bore, nor bowed before, the deadlier face
 of want.

What lack we here of show and form that lure your
 kerns to death?
Not serried bands, nor sinewy hands, nor music's martial breath;
And if we broke the slavish yoke our suppliant race
 endure,
No robbers we—but chivalry—the Army of the Poor
Out on ye now, ye Lordly crew, that do your betters
 wrong—
We are no base and braggart mob, but merciful and
 strong.

Your henchmen vain, your vassal train, would fly our
    first defiance ;
In us—in our strong, tranquil breasts—abides your sole
    reliance.

Ay! keep them all, castle and hall, coffers and costly
    jewels—
Keep your vile gain, and in its train the passions that it
    fuels.
We envy not your lordly lot—its bloom or its decay-
    ance ;
But ye *have* that we claim as ours—our right in long
    abeyance :
Leisure to live, leisure to love, leisure to taste our free-
    dom—
Oh! suff'ring poor, oh! patient poor, how bitterly you
    need them!
"Ever to moil, ever to toil," that is your social charter,
And city slave or rustic serf, the TOILER is its martyr.

Where Frank and Tuscan shed their sweat the goodly
    crop is theirs—
If Norway's toil make rich the soil, she eats the fruit she
    rears—
O'er Maine's green sward there rules no lord, saving the
    Lord on high ;
But we are serfs in our own land—proud masters, tell us
    why ?
The German burgher and his men, brother with bro-
    thers live,
While toil must wait without *your* gate what gracious
    crusts you give.
Long in your sight, for our own right, like stricken slaves
    we bend ;—
Why did we bow ? why do we now ?—My masters, this
    must end.

Perish the past—a generous land is this fair land of ours,
And enmity may no man see between its Towns and
    Towers.

Come, join our bands—here take our hands—now shame
    on him that lingers,
Merchant or Peer, you have no fear from labour's blis-
    tered fingers.
Come, join at last—perish the past—its traitors, its se-
    ceders—
Proud names and old, frank hearts and bold, come join
    and be our Leaders.
*But know, ye lords, that be your swords with us or with
    our Wronger,*
*Heaven be our guide, we Toilers bide this lot of shame no
    longer !*

---

## THE DREAM OF JOHN MAC DONNELL.

### TRANSLATED FROM THE IRISH.

### BY JAMES CLARENCE MANGAN.

[John Mac Donnell, usually called Mac Donnell *Claragh*, from his family residence, was a native of the County of Cork, and may be classed among the first of the purely Irish poets of the last century. He was born in 1691, and died in 1754. His poems are remarkable for their energy, their piety of tone, and the patriotic spirit they every where manifest. The following is one of them, and deserves to be regarded as a very curious topographical "Jacobite relic."

I LAY in unrest—old thoughts of pain,
    That I struggled in vain to smother,
Like midnight spectres haunted my brain—
    Dark fantasies chased each other;
When, lo! a Figure—who might it be?—
    A tall fair figure stood near me!
Who might it be? An unreal Banshee?
    Or an angel sent to cheer me?

Though years have rolled since then, yet now
  My memory thrillingly lingers
On her awful charms, her waxen brow,
  Her pale translucent fingers ;—
Her eyes that mirrored a wonder-world,
  Her mien of unearthly mildness,
And her waving raven tresses that curled
  To the ground in beautiful wildness.

"Whence comest thou, Spirit?" I asked, methought,
  "Thou art not one of the Banished?"
Alas, for me! she answered nought,
  But rose aloft and vanished ;
And a radiance, like to a glory, beamed
  In the light she left behind her,
Long time I wept, and at last medreamed
  I left my shieling to find her.

And first I turned to the thunderous North,
  To Gruagach's mansion kingly ;
Untouching the earth, I then sped forth
  To Inver-lough, and the shingly
And shining strand of the fishful Erne,
  And thence to Cruachan the golden,
Of whose resplendent palace ye learn
  So many a marvel olden!

I saw the Mourna's billows flow—
  I passed the walls of Shenady,
And stood in the hero-thronged Ardroe,
  Embosked amid greenwoods shady ;
And visited that proud pile that stands
  Above the Boyne's broad waters,
Where Ængus dwells with his warrior-bands
  And the fairest of Ulster's daughters.

To the halls of Mac Lir, to Creevroe's height,
  To Tara, the glory of Erin,
To the fairy palace that glances bright
  On the peak of the blue Cnocfeerin,

I vainly hied.  I went west and east—
  I travelled seaward and shoreward—
But thus was I greeted in field and at feast—
  "Thy way lies onward and foreward!"

At last I reached, I wist not how,
  The royal towers of Ival,
Which, under the cliff's gigantic brow,
  Still rise without a rival;
And here were Thomond's chieftains all,
  With armour, and swords, and lances,
And here sweet music filled the hall,
  And damsels charmed with dances.

And here, at length, on a silvery throne,
  Half seated, half reclining,
With forehead white as the marble stone,
  And garments so starrily shining,
And features beyond the poet's pen—
  The sweetest, saddest features—
Appeared before me once agen,
  That fairest of Living Creatures!

"Draw near, O mortal!" she said, with a sigh,
  "And hear my mournful story!
The Guardian-Spirit of ERIN am I,
  But dimmed is mine ancient glory.
My priests are banished, my warriors wear
  No longer Victory's garland;
And my Child,* my Son, my beloved Heir,
  Is an exile in a far     !"

I heard no more—I saw no more—
  The bands of slumber were broken;
And palace and hero, and river and shore,
  Had vanished, and left no token.
Dissolved was the spell that had bound my will,
  And my fancy thus for a season;
But a sorrow therefore hangs over me still,
  Despite of the teachings of Reason!

* Charles Stuart.

## THE WEXFORD INSURGENT.

#### TRANSLATED FROM THE IRISH.

THE heroes of Wexford have burst through their chains
And the voice of the freeman is loud o'er her plains—
The Sassanachs are broken, their horsemen have fled,
And the pride of their host on the mountain lie dead.

For roused is the blood of the bold *Shilmaleer*,
The pride of the conflict when foemen are near—
And the heroes of Bargy and Bantry are there,
In the shock ever foremost, in flight in the rere.

Oh! soon will the hearths of the traitors be lone,
And their halls but re-echo the shriek and the groan,
And the red flame shall burst thro' their roofs to the
    sky,
For the hour of our freedom and vengeance is nigh.

The men of the mountain are down in the vale,
And the flags of Shelburny are loose to the gale—
And tho' gentle the Forth, yet her sons never slight,
For the mildest in peace are oft boldest in fight.

The cold-blooded Sassanach is low on the hill,
Like the red rock he presses, as lone and as chill—
There, pulseless and cold, the pale beams of the moon
Show the deep-riven breast of the fallen dragoon.

And low lies his charger, his bosom all torn,
And from the dark helmet the horse hair is shorn,
And the hearts of the great, and the brave, and the
    proud,
Have been trampled in death when the battle was loud.

Oh! long in fair England each maiden may mourn—
The pride of her bosom will never return;
His heart's blood is scattered—his last prayer is said—
And the dark raven flaps his wild wing o'er the dead

Yes, long she may call him from battle in vain—
The sight of her lover she ne'er shall regain:
All cold is his bosom, and crimson his brow,
And the night wind is sighing its dirge o'er him now.

## THE ORANGEMAN'S WIFE.

### BY CAROLL MALONE.

I WANDER by the limpid shore,
   When fields and flowrets bloom;
But, oh! my heart is sad and sore—
   My soul is sunk in gloom—
All day I cry ohone! ohone!
   I weep from night till morn—
I wish that I were dead and gone,
   Or never had been born.

My father dwelt beside Tyrone,
   And with him children five;
But I to Charlemont had gone,
   At service there to live.
O brothers fond! O sister dear!
   How ill I paid your love!
O father! father! how I fear
   To meet thy soul above!

My mother left us long ago,—
   A lovely corpse was she,—
But we had longer days of wo
   In this sad world to be.
My weary days will soon be done—
   I pine in grief forlorn;
I wish that I were dead and gone,
   Or never had been born.

It was the year of ninety-eight;
  The wreckers came about;
They burned my father's stack of wheat,
  And drove my brothers out;
They forced my sister to their lust—
  God grant my father rest!
For the captain of the wreckers thrust
  A bayonet through his breast.

It was a dreadful, dreadful year;
  And I was blindly led,
In love, and loneliness, and fear,
  A loyal man to wed;
And still my heart is his alone,
  It breaks, but cannot turn:
I wish that I were dead and gone,
  Or never had been born.

Next year we lived in quiet love,
  And kissed our infant boy;
And peace had spread her wings above
  Our dwelling at the Moy.
And then my wayworn brothers came
  To share our peace and rest;
And poor lost Rose, to hide her shame
  And sorrow in my breast.

They came, but soon they turned and fled—
  Preserve my soul, O God!
It was my husband's hand, they said,
  That shed my father's blood.
All day I cry ohone! ohone!
  I weep from night till morn;
And oh, that I were dead and gone,
  Or never had been born!

## THE IRISH CHIEFS.

#### BY CHARLES GAVAN DUFFY.

Oh! to have lived like an IRISH CHIEF, when hearts
  were fresh and true,
And a manly thought, like a pealing bell, would quicken
  them through and through;
And the seed of a gen'rous hope right soon to a fiery
  action grew,
And men would have scorned to talk, and talk, and
  never a deed to do.
  Oh! the iron grasp,
  And the kindly clasp,
  And the laugh so fond and gay;
  And the roaring board,
  And the ready sword,
  Were the types of that vanished day.

Oh! to have lived as Brian lived, and to die as Brian
  died;
His land to win with the sword, and smile,\* as a war-
  rior wins his bride.
To knit its force in a kingly host, and rule it with
  kingly pride,
And still in the girt of its guardian swords over victor
  fields to ride;
  And when age was past,
  And when death came fast,
  To look with a softened eye
  On a happy race
  Who had loved his face,
  And to die as a king should die.

---

\* Our great Brian is called an usurper, inasmuch as he combined, by force and policy, the scattered and jealous powers of the island into one sovereignty, and ruled it himself, by the true Divine right of being the fittest —"—

Oh! to have lived dear Owen's life—to live for a solemn
    end,
To strive for the ruling strength and skill God's saints
    to the Chosen send;
And to come at length, with that holy strength, the
    bondage of fraud to rend,
And pour the light of God's freedom in where Tyrants
    and Slaves were denned;
    And to bear the brand
    With an equal hand,
  Like a soldier of Truth and Right.
    And, oh! Saints, to die,
    While our flag flew high,
  Nor to look on its fall or flight


Oh, to have lived as Grattan lived, in the glow of his
    manly years,
To thunder again those iron words that smite like the
    clash of spears;
Once more to blend for a holy end, our peasants, and
    priests, and peers,
Till England raged, like a baffled fiend, at the tramp of
    our Volunteers.
    And, oh! best of all,
    Far rather to fall
  (With a blesseder fate than he,)
    On a conqu'ring field,
    Than one right to yield,
  Of the Island so proud and free!


Yet, scorn to cry on the days of old, when hearts were
    fresh and true,
If hearts be weak, oh! chiefly *then* the Missioned their
    work must do;
Nor wants our day its own fit way, the want is in *you*
    and *you*;
For these eyes have seen as kingly a King as ever dear
    Erin knew.

   And with Brian's will,
   And with Owen's skill,
  And with glorious Grattan's love,
   He had freed us soon—
   But death darkened his noon,
  And he sits with the saints above.

Oh! could you live as Davis lived—kind Heaven be us
  led!
With an eye to guide, and a hand to rule, and a calm
  and kingly head,
And a heart from whence, like a Holy Well, the soul of
  his land was fed.
No need to cry on the days of old that your holiest hope
  be sped.
   Then scorn to pray
   For a bye-past day—
  The whine of the sightless dumb!
   To the true and wise
   Let a king arise,
  And a holier day is come!

# MISCELLANEOUS BALLADS.

## THE SAINT'S TENANT.

### BY THOMAS FURLONG.

[This painful ballad illustrates a system of bigotry, injustice, and oppression which, I believe, has almost entirely ceased to exist in this country. Education is not now to be purchased at so great a risk, and at such a cost. The means at present available, or about to be made available, may not be as perfect as some of us would wish; but we should not forget the unspeakable danger and suffering to soul and body from which, in this respect, at least, the people have escaped. I would wish to refer the reader to another poem on this subject, entitled "The Penal Days," which I have placed third in this division.— I have not inserted these poems, however, or any other in the volume, on political grounds. Literary merit and Irish feeling, no matter from what side of the Boyne it came, have been the only test; my object being to present to the reader such a collection of IRISH BALLADS as would be valuable in a literary point of view, and which would not be altogether useless to the historian. or to the student of our customs, our sufferings, or our character.—ED.]

AROUND the hills I ranged all day,
   'Twas a spring's day, not warm though fine;
   The sun himself became my clock,
I marked him with attentive eye,
And saw him drooping in the sky.

Then downwards I did bend my way,
For still, whate'er some wild ones say,
  The barren heath or mossy rock
  Can't furnish much whereon to dine.
'Twas a spring's day, the birds were seen
  Peeping by stealth from bush and spray,
The fields all round looked fresh and green,
  And then to hear the small birds sing,
  It was, in sooth, a cheering thing.
From childhood among birds I've been,
  Catching their notes from brake and bough,
To me their songs were ever dear;
But there was something o'er me here,
In the soft air or sky so clear,
Some spell or charm mixt with the scene,
  That gave those songs new beauty now.

Oh! who, thought I, would not be gay,
  Enjoying this sweet hour like me;
A man that moment crossed my way,
  Who showed small sign of gaiety.
Down o'er his brow his hat he drew,
  I saw him turn and wipe his eyes;
That he in trouble was, I knew,
  But knew not whence it might arise.

  "Good friend," said I, "what makes thee weep,
What may your cross or trouble be?"
"Trouble enough, I have," quoth he,
  "I poils my meals, it breaks my sleep,
No chance on any side I see,
My lot through lif is misery.
  Yet it is weak to yield to grief,
For hours, for days, this cheek or eye
Have seldom been a moment dry;
'Tis, as I say, a foolish thing
To cry when tears no aid can bring;
Still do I think that when they fall,
They ease this wretched head withal,
  And give the heavy heart relief.

" Within that cozy little cot.
   That by my lady's gate appears;
Sometimes contented with my lot,
Sometimes at ease, and sometimes not:
   I've lingered on for ten long years.
I laboured sorely through the day,
And got but sorry, scanty pay;
My wife she was a struggler too,
And did as much as wife could do;
Still did we find it hard indeed
The children and ourselves to feed;
But yet we should have been content,
As we stood clear of tax or rent;
We had the little cottage free,
For of the gate we kept the key.


" And as the years all slowly fled,
For many a guest that gate I spread;
For many a visitor came there,
   Fine gentle folks of each degree,
Sea-officers with careless air,
   And rosy squires all blunt and free,
And captains and gay cornets too,
In their rich dress of red or blue;
And such I still was glad to see,
For they had a cheerful look of glee;
They bore no made-up look of grace,
Where the bad heart belied the face;
Nor gloomy airs nor bows demure—
In short, they didn't teaze the poor,
Nor bring them harm nor get them blame,
Nor wrong them in religion's name.


"Oh, 'twas for us a heavy day,
When the squires and captains kept away,
And the sleekheaded race came in,
To prate of sanctity and sin;
To rave of darkness and of light,
And eat and drink from morn till night;

To grunt and groan around my lady,
   To turn her cheerfulness to gall,
To have vile stories ever ready,
   To set her mind against us all.
'Twas in this way the canting clan
Their work of godliness began.

'Each child, each fool, about the hall,
   Got texts quite pat for every thing;
New birth—new light—conversion—call,
   Seemed ever in one's ears to ring.
My wife and I kept from the place,
We wanted not this extra grace;
We longed not for the saints' debating,
We cared not for mere children's prating,
Who settled points that, as we're told,
Puzzled the wisest heads of old;
We wished in quietness to stay,
And tread our own plain level way;
To leave new-fangled creeds untried,
And die as those before us died.

"My two poor boys at school had been,
   And for their time got on quite well:
The master was a worthy man,
   One who much better days had seen;
   But when misfortune on him fell,
Beside the chapel on the green
He took a cottage, and began
To train those children who could bring
From week to week the smallest thing;
A very trifle satisfied him,
And none of what he asked denied him.

"My lady built a Sunday school,
   At least she lent her aid;
And there they fixt a solemn fool,
   Who groaned, and preached, and prayed.
Perhaps 'tis wrong the name I gave,
He was, I think, less fool than knave;

He canted well, and soon stood high
In favour in my lady's eye;
She told her tenantry at large
To give their children to his charge;
It cost the creatures many a tear,
But they were forced to yield through fear;
What can a poor dependent do,
With certain ruin full in view;
If even one murmuring word is spoken,
Or one capricious order broken?

"I sent my boys with heavy heart,
  Their chance withal to try;
I knew I played a guilty part,
  But what resource had I?
I knew their faith was placed in danger,
By listening to this canting stranger;
To me their ancient faith was dear,
But if my lady chanced to hear
One lingering growl, for me or mine
  There was no choice, no prospect left,
But friendless in some ditch to pine,
  Of shelter, food, and work bereft;
This was what baulked me through the past,
And see to this 'tis come at last.

"We were not long in finding out
What the new teacher was about;
  Of writing, sums, or figures, he
Appeared to take but little care;
  His study was divinity.
He'd scripture—scripture—every where,
  He crammed it in the rule of three;
He made it chime with tret and tare,
The rule of three was not with him
  As with the world—the golden rule;
He had a notion in his head
That truth and godliness were dead;
He thought his pupil's faith burned dim
  And he did call his little school

By a strange name—'twas, as I guess,
A roaring 'howling wilderness,'
Where the great fiend might freely prowl,
And pounce upon each 'bat and owl;'
For so he styled those little sinners
Who were in grace not e'en beginners.

"He got this maggot in his brain,
It bit him o'er and o'er again;
It urged him to his holy work,
To tear the beast, the Pope, and Turk.
Each urchin in his favour grew,
Who soured him in this pious view;
The best boy's merit was but small,
Unless he learned to twist St. Paul;
Or from his book had morsels ready
To throw at the old Scarlet Lady;
For by this name did he presume
To call the blessed Church of Rome.
But they were in his chosen class,
Who mocked the priest and staid from mass.
Who threw their parents' creed aside,
And took My Lady for their guide.
Of these my eldest boy was one—
I can't say how his change begun—
But saw it soon—one evening he
Spoke, as I thought, too flippantly
Of holy things: I checked his tongue,
But he would not be silent long;
He growled, and in the cant of school
Called me a superstitious fool;
And then he laughed all loud and gay,
 To see me for the moment stare:
I stared indeed, and cursed the day
 That left him in the Swaddler's care.
Next morn, more mischief to prevent,
His brother and himself were sent
To the old school upon the green,
Where both of them at first had been;

I did not heed my danger then,
　Nor see the harm that I was doing;
But quarrel once with holy men,
　And soon they'll bring about your ruin;
Revenge is theirs, if touched or crost,
At least I found so to my cost.

"Ay, Sir! before two days were gone
My punishment was settled on.
The holy teacher lost no time
In blazoning forth my heinous crime;
Down to our door the steward came,
And told me, in his lady's name,
That though the snow was on the ground,
　Though chill and frosty was the air,
By me new quarters must be found,
　To go at once I must prepare,
　For I could stop no longer there;
'I'm sorry for your loss,' quoth he
(I thought he spoke it sneeringly),
'But if you wish employment still,
　Or shelter from the wintry blast,
Why, yield you to my lady's will,
　And she may pardon all that's past.
Your best and surest way would be
　The teacher's favour to obtain;
Stick not so hard to Popery,
　But bring the youngsters back again;
And with them let him take his way—
What signifies it how they pray?
This you must do, and more than this,
For things half done are done amiss;
The boys must change, nor they alone,
A change must by yourself be shown.
My lady bids you think with dread
Of the sad life you've lately led:
Up to the hall you must repair,
Each evening at the hour of prayer,
And bring your children and your wife,
To hear betimes the words of life,

And learn what priests have never taught,
Or never dwelt on as they ought;
By this, perhaps, you gain your end,
You hold your place and keep your friend.
This is my counsel, as I live,
In friendship I this counsel give ;
But if you, like a stubborn dunce,
  Will fling this good advice aside,
Why in Heaven's name, then, be at once
    The comforts of starvation tried ;
Go forth, and wish, perhaps too late,
For the warm cottage at the gate.'


" 'Then let starvation come,' said I,
' Heaven in its hour will help the poor—
We'll beg our way from door to door,
And if no food we can procure,
    The worst that waits us is to die.
But, oh ! it is not fair to try
Or tempt a struggling man like me
To practise vile hypocrisy.
No ! let my lady's anger fall
Upon me—I can bear it all :
Still to my father's faith I'll keep,
And take this boy, this poor stray sheep,
From where the wolves grin greedily '


" 'Father, mistake me not,' said he,
' I cannot, will not dwell with thee ;
I may not walk upon thy path,
When Heaven thus marks thee in its wrath
Why should I grope in darkness still,
When it has been the Lord's good will
To bless me with a ray of light,
And make me sinless, pure and bright ?
From Satan's power I now stand free,
From that and hell-born Popery ;
To my good teacher I shall go,
And he will be my friend, I know.'

"The stripling rose, he reached his hat,
In mute astonishment I sat,
And saw him as, with saintly face,
He led the steward from the place:
No word of censure I let fall—
I could not—but I looked it all.

"They turned us out, on the road side
In an old shed we dwell:
With food, with firing unsupplied;
Of clothes and bedding nearly bare,
We shivering sit, and suffer there
Much more than I could tell,
And yet I feel I acted well;
My father's faith I held secure—
And though I'm shelterless and poor,
I would not change that faith to buy
All that these kingdoms could supply
God be my friend!"—"Amen!" said I.

## LAMENT FOR THE SONS OF USNACH.

### BY SAMUEL FERGUSON, M.R.I.A.

["Then was there no man in the host of Ulster that could be found who would put the sons of Usnach to death, so loved were they of the people and nobles. But in the house of Conor was one called Maini, Rough Hand, son of the King of Lochlin, and Naisi had slain his father and two brothers, and he undertook to be their executioner. So the sons of Usnach were there slain, and the men of Ulster, when they beheld their death, sent forth their heavy shouts of sorrow and lamentation. Then Deirdre fell down beside their bodies, wailing and weeping, and she tore her hair in garments, and bestowed kisses on their lifeless lips, and bitterly bemoaned them. And a grave was opened for them, and Deirdre, standing by it, with her hair dishevelled, and shedding tears abundantly, chanted their funeral song."*]

THE lions of the hill are gone,
And I am left alone—alone—

* Hibernian Nights' Entertainments, University Magazine, vol. lr.
p. 686.

Dig the grave both wide and deep,
For I am sick, and fain would sleep!

The falcons of the wood are flown,
And I am left alone—alone—
Dig the grave both deep and wide,
And let us slumber side by side.

The dragons of the rock are sleeping,
Sleep that wakes not for our weeping
Dig the grave, and make it ready,
Lay me on my true-love's body.

Lay their spears and bucklers bright
By the warriors' sides aright;
Many a day the three before me
On their linked bucklers bore me.

Lay upon the low grave floor,
'Neath each head, the blue claymore,
Many a time the noble three
Reddened these blue blades for me.

Lay the collars, as is meet,
Of their greyhounds at their feet;
Many a time for me have they
Brought the tall red deer to bay.

In the falcon's jesses throw,
Hook and arrow, line and bow;
Ne'er again, by stream or plain,
Shall the gentle woodsmen go.

Sweet companions, ye were ever—
Harsh to me, your sister, never;
Woods and wilds, and misty vallies,
Were with you as good's a palace.

Oh. to hear my true love singing,
Sweet as sound of trumpets ringing;
Like the sway of ocean swelling
Rolled his deep voice round our dwelling

Oh! to hear the echoes pealing
Round our green and fairy sheeling,
When the three, with soaring chorus,
Passed the silent skylark o'er us.

Echo now, sleep, morn and even—
Lark alone enchant the heaven!—
Ardan's lips are scant of breath,
Naisi's tongue is cold in death.

Stag, exult on glen and mountain—
Salmon, leap from loch to fountain—
Heron, in the free air warm ye—
Usnach's sons no more will harm ye!

Erin's stay no more you are,
Rulers of the ridge of war!
Never more 'twill be your fate
To keep the beam of battle straight!

Wo is me! by fraud and wrong,
Traitors false and tyrants strong,
Fell clan Usnach, bought and sold,
For Barach's feast and Conor's gold!

Wo to Eman, roof and wall!—
Wo to Red Branch, hearth and hall!—
Tenfold wo and black dishonor
To the foul and false clan Conor!

Dig the grave both wide and deep,
Sick I am, and fain would sleep!
Dig the grave and make it ready,
Lay me on my true-love's body!

## THE PENAL DAYS.

[" In Scotland what a work have the four-and-twenty letters to show for themselves! The natural enemies of vice, and folly, and slavery; the great sowers, but the still greater weeders of the human soil."— *John Philpot Curran.*]

In that dark time of cruel wrong, when on our coun-
    try's breast,
A dreary load, a ruthless code, with wasting terrors
    prest—
Our gentry stript of land and clan, sent exiles o'er the
    main,
To turn the scales on foreign fields for foreign monarchs'
    gain—
Our people trod like vermin down, all fenceless flung to
    sate
Extortion, lust, and brutal whim, and rancorous bigot
    hate—
Our priesthood tracked from cave to hut, like felons
    chased and lashed,
And from their ministering hands the lifted chalice
    dashed;
In that black time of law-wrought crime, of stifling wo
    and thrall,
There stood supreme one foul device, one engine worse
    than all.

Him whom they wished to keep a slave, they sought to
    make a brute—
They banned the light of heaven—they bade instruc-
    tion's voice be mute
God's second priest—the Teacher—sent to feed men's
    mind with lore—
They marked a price upon his head, as on the priest's
    before.
Well—well they knew that never, face to face beneath
    the sky,

Could tyranny and knowledge meet, but one of them
  should die :
That lettered slaves will link their might until their
  murmurs grow
To that imperious thunder-peal which despots quail to
  know ;
That men who learn will learn their strength—the weak-
  ness of their lords—
Till all the bonds that gird them round are snapt like
  Sampson's cords.
This well they knew, and called the power of ignorance
  to aid :
So might, they deemed, an abject race of soulless serfs
  be made—
When Irish memories, hopes, and thoughts, were wi-
  thered, branch and stem—
A race of abject, soulless serfs, to hew and draw for
  them.

Ah, God is good and nature strong—they let not thus
  decay
The seeds that deep in Irish breasts of Irish feeling lay,
Still sun and rain made emerald green the loveliest
  fields on earth,
And gave the type of deathless hope, the little sham-
  rock, birth ;
Still faithful to their Holy Church, her direst straits
  among,
To one another faithful still, the priests and people
  clung,
And Christ was worshipped, and received with trem-
  bling haste and fear,
In field and shed, with posted scouts to warn of blood-
  hounds near ;
Still, crouching 'neath the sheltering hedge, or stretched
  on mountain fern,
The teacher and his pupils met, feloniously—to learn ;
Still round the peasant's heart of hearts his darling
  music twined,
A fount of Irish sobs or smiles in every note enshrined

And still beside the smouldering turf were fond tradi-
    tions told
Of heavenly saints and princely chiefs—the power and
    faith of old

Deep lay the seeds, yet rankest weeds sprang mingled—
    could they fail?
For what were freedom's blessed worth, if slavery
    wrought not bale?
As thrall, and want, and ignorance, still deep and deeper
    grew,
What marvel weakness, gloom, and strife fell dark
    amongst us too,
And servile thoughts, that measure not the inborn wealth
    of man—
And servile cringe, and subterfuge to 'scape our master's
    ban.—
And drunkenness—our sense of woe a little while to
    steep—
And aimless feud, and murderous plot—oh, one could
    pause and weep!
'Mid all the darkness, faith in Heaven still shone, a
    saving ray,
And Heaven o'er our redemption watched, and chose its
    own good day.
Two men were sent us—one for years, with Titan strength
    of soul,
To beard our foes, to peal our wrongs, to band us and
    control.
The other at a later time, on gentler mission came,
To make our noblest glory spring from out our saddest
    shame!
On all our wondrous, upward course hath Heaven its
    finger set,
And we—but, oh, my countrymen, there's much before
    us yet!

How sorrowful the useless powers our glorious Island
    yields—
Our countless havens desolate, our waste of barren
    fields,

The all unused mechanic might our rushing streams
    afford,
The buried treasures of our mines, our sea's unvalued
    hoard!
But, oh, there is one piteous waste whence all the rest
    have grown,
One worst neglect, the mind of man left desert and
    unsown.
Send KNOWLEDGE forth to scatter wide, and deep to cast
    its seeds.
The nurse of energy and hope, of manly thoughts and
    deeds.
Let it go forth: right soon will spring those forces in its
    train
That vanquish Nature's stubborn strength, that rifle
    earth and main—
Itself a nobler harvest far than Autumn tints with
    gold,
A higher wealth, a surer gain than wave and mine
    enfold.
Let it go forth unstained, and purged from Pride's un-
    holy leaven,
With fearless forehead raised to Man, but humbly bent
    to Heaven;
Deep let it sink in Irish hearts the story of their isle,
And waken thoughts of tenderest love, and burning
    wrath the while;
And press upon us, one by one, the fruits of English
    sway,
And blend the wrongs of bygone times with this our fight
    to-day;
And show our Father's constancy by truest instinct led,
To loathe and battle with the power that on their sub-
    stance fed;
And let it place beside our own the world's vast page, to
    tell
That never lived the nation yet could rule another well.
Thus, thus our cause shall gather strength; no feeling
    vague and blind,
But stamped by passion on the heart, by reason on the
    mind.

Let it go forth—a mightier foe to England's power than all
The rifles of America—the armaments of Gaul!
It *shall* go forth, and wo to them that bar or thwart its way—
'Tis God's own light—all Heavenly bright—we care not who says nay.

---

## CAROLAN AND BRIDGET CRUISE.

### BY SAMUEL LOVER.

[It is related of Carolan, the Irish bard, that when deprived of sight, and after the lapse of twenty years, he recognized his first love by the touch of her hand. The lady's name was Bridget Cruise; and though not a pretty name, it deserves to be recorded, as belonging to the woman who could inspire such a passion.]

"True love can ne'er forget;
Fondly as when we met,
Dearest, I love thee yet,
   My darling one!"
Thus sung a minstrel gay
His sweet impassion'd lay,
Down by the ocean's spray
   At set of sun;
But wither'd was the minstrel's sight,
Morn to him was dark as night,
Yet his heart was full of light;
   As he thus his lay begun.

"True love can ne'er forget
Fondly as when we met,
Dearest, I love thee yet,
   My darling one!

'Long years are past and o'er,
Since from this fatal shore,
Cold hearts and cold winds bore
　　My love from me."
Scarcely the minstrel spoke,
When quick, with flashing stroke,
A boat's light oar the silence broke
　　O'er the sea;

Soon upon her native strand
Doth a lovely lady land,
With the minstrel's love-taught hand
　　Did o'er his wild harp run:
"True love can ne'er forget;
Fondly as when we met,
Dearest, I love thee yet,
　　My darling one!"
Where the minstrel sat alone,
There, that lady fair hath gone,
Within his hand she placed her own,
　　The bard dropp'd on his knee;

From his lips soft blessings came,
He kiss'd her hand with truest flame,
In trembling tones he named—*her* name
　　Though he could not see;
But oh!—the touch the bard could tell
Of that dear hand, remember'd well,
Ah!—by many a secret spell
　　Can true love find her own!
For true love can ne'er forget;
Fondly as when they met;
He loved his lady yet,
　　His darling one

## THE STREAMS.

### BY MRS. DOWNING.

[This poem is taken from a volume entitled "Scraps from the Mountains, by Christabel," published in Dublin in 1840. It contains many beautiful pieces, in which Mrs. Downing has succeeded in uniting much of the grace and harmony of Mrs. Hemans, to the tenderness and passion of L. E. L. What is still better, they are thoroughly Irish in sentiment and expression.]

THE streams, the dancing streams,
  How they roll and shine!
Like youth's fairest dreams,
  When youth is most divine;
Clearness where their bed is,
  'Mid pebbles in glossy ranks,
Brightness on their eddies,
  Blossoms on their banks.

Look within the valley,
  Many a charm is there;
The winding shaded alley,
  The woodbine glist'ning fair,
The berries' crimson flush,
  The wild birds' cadence low,
But chief of all, the gush
  Of the streamlet's singing flow.

Stand beneath the mountains,
  And down each craggy side,
From their secret fountain,
  See lines of silver glide—
Mark how the ripples fling
  Their sparkles round, and say
If there is anything
  More beautiful than they

List in night's deep hushing,
   The season time of dreams,
What are these come rushing?
   The troubled, sleepless streams!
Now their waters flashing,
   Like starry-spangled hairs—
Rolling, bounding, dashing—
   What music like to theirs?

Oh! in the sheltered glen,
   Or on the hill side fair,
When spring flowers bloom, or when
   The summer birds are there
In all that we may see,
   'Neath morn's or evening's beams,
Can aught in nature be
   More lovely than the streams?

---

## IRISH MARY.

### BY JOHN BANIM.

FAR away from Erin's strand,
   And valleys wide and sounding waters,
Still she is, in every land,
   One of Erin's real daughters:
Oh! to meet her here is like
   A dream of home and natal mountains.
On our hearts their voices strike—
   We hear the gushing of their fountains!
Yes! our Irish Mary dear!
   Our own, our real Irish Mary!
A flower of home, fresh blooming come,
   Art thou to us our Irish Mary!

Round about us here we see
   Bright eyes like hers, and sunny faces,
Charming all!—if all were free
   Of foreign airs, of borrowed graces.
Mary's eye it flashes truth !
   And Mary's spirit, Mary's nature,
"Irish Lady," fresh in youth,
   Have beamed o'er every look and feature!
Yes! our Irish Mary dear!
   When *La Tournure* doth make us weary,
We have you, to turn unto
   For native grace, our Irish Mary.

Sighs of home!—her Erin's songs
   O'er all their songs we love to listen;
Tears of home!—her Erin's wrongs
   Subdue our kindred eyes to glisten!
Oh! should woe to gloom consign
   The clear fire-side of love and honour,
You will see a holier sign
   Of Irish Mary bright upon her!
Yes! our Irish Mary dear
   Will light that home, though e'er so dreary,
Shining still o'er clouds of ill,
   Sweet star of life, our Irish Mary!

---

## THE LAST FRIENDS.

### BY FRANCES BROWN.

[One of the United Irishmen, who lately returned to his country, after many years of exile, being asked what had induced him to revisit Ireland when all his friends were gone, he answered, "I came back to see the mountains."]

I CAME to my country, but not with the hope
   That brightened my youth like the cloud-lighting bow
For the region of soul that seemed mighty to cope
   With time and with fortune, had fled from me now;

And love, that illumined my wanderings of yore,
  Hath perished, and left but a weary regret
For the star that can rise on my midnight no more—
  But the hills of my country they welcome me yet!

The hue of their verdure was fresh with me still,
  When my path was afar by the Tanais' lone track;
From the wide-spreading deserts and ruins, that fill
  The land of old story, they summoned me back;
They rose on my dreams through the shades of the west,
  They breathed upon sands which the dew never wet,
For the echoes were hushed in the home I loved best—
  But I knew that the mountains would welcome me yet!

The dust of my kindred is scattered afar,
  They lie in the desert, the wild, and the wave,
For serving the strangers through wandering and war,
  The isle of their memory could grant them no grave.
And I, I return with the memory of years,
  Whose hope rose so high though in sorrow it set;
They have left on my soul but the trace of their tears—
  But our mountains remember their promises yet!

Oh! where are the brave hearts that bounded of old,
  And where are the faces my childhood hath seen?
For fair brows are furrowed, and hearts have grown cold
  But our streams are still bright, and our hills are still green;
Ay, green as they rose to the eyes of my youth,
  When brothers in heart in their shadows we met;
And the hills have no memory of sorrow or death,
  For their summits are sacred to liberty yet!

Like ocean retiring, the morning mists now
  Roll back from the mountains that girdle our land;
And sunlight encircles each heath-covered brow
  For which time had no furrow and tyrants no brand;

Oh, thus let it be with the hearts of the isle,
  Efface the dark seal that oppression hath let;
Give back the lost glory again to the soil,
  For the hills of my country remember it yet·

---

## THE IRISH EXILES.

#### A CHRISTMAS CAROL.

### BY MARTIN MAC DERMOTT.

WHEN round the festive Christmas board, or by the
    Christmas hearth,
That glorious mingled draught is pour'd—wine, melody,
    and mirth!
When friends long absent tell, low-toned, their joys and
    sorrows o'er,
And hand grasps hand. and eyelids fill, and lips meet
    lips once more—
Oh! in that hour 'twere kindly done, some woman's
    voice would say—
"Forget not those who're sad to-night—poor exiles, far
    away!"

Alas, for them! this morning's sun saw many a moist
    eye pour
Its gushing love, with longings vain, the waste Atlantic
    o'er,
And when he turned his lion-eye this ev'ning from the
    West,
The Indian shores were lined with those who watched
    his couched crest;
But not to share his glory, then, or gladden in his ray,
*They* bent their gaze upon his path—those exiles, far
    away!

It was—oh! how the heart will cheat! because they
   thought, beyond
His glowing couch lay that Green Isle of which their
   hearts were fond;
And fancy brought old scenes of home into each welling
   eye,
And through each breast pour'd many a thought that
   filled it like a sigh!
'Twas then—'twas then, all warm with love, they knelt
   them down to pray
For Irish homes and kith and kin—poor exiles far
   away!

And then the mother blest her son, the lover blest the
   maid,
And then the soldier was a child, and wept the whilst
   he prayed,
And then the student's pallid cheek flushed red as summer rose,
And patriot souls forgot their grief to weep for Erin's
   woes;
And, oh! but then warm vows were breathed, that come
   what might or may,
They'd right the suffering isle they loved—those exiles,
   far away!

And some there were around the board, like loving brothers met,
The few and fond and joyous hearts that never can forget;
They pledged—" The girls we left at home, God bless
   them!" and they gave.
" The memory of our absent friends, the tender and the
   brave!"
Then up, erect, with nine times nine—hip, hip, hip—
   hurrah!
Drank—" Erin slantha gal go bragh!"\* those exiles
   far away.

* Erin slantha gal go bragh.

Then, oh! to hear the sweet old strains of Irish music rise,
Like gushing memories of home, beneath far foreign skies,
Beneath the spreading calabash, beneath the trellised vine,
The bright Italian myrtle bower, or dark Canadian pine—
Oh! don't these old familiar tones—now sad, and now so gay—
Speak out your very, very hearts—poor exiles, far away!


But, Heavens! how many sleep afar, all heedless of these strains—
Tired wanderers! who sought repose through Europe's battle plains—
In strong, fierce, headlong fight they fell—as ships go down in storms—
They fell—and *human* whirlwinds swept across their shattered forms!
No shroud, but glory, wrapt them round; nor pray'r nor tear had they—
Save the wandering winds and the heavy clouds—poor exiles far away!


And might the singer claim a sigh, he, too, could tell how tost
Upon the stranger's dreary shore, his heart's best hopes were lost—
How he, too, pined, to hear the tones of friendship greet his ear,
And pined, to walk the river side, to youthful musing dear,
And pined, with yearning silent love, amongst *his own* to stay—
Alas! it is so sad to be an exile, far away!

Then, oh! when round the Christmas board, or by the
    Christmas hearth,
That glorious mingled draught is poured—wine, melody,
    and mirth!
When friends long absent tell, low-toned, their joys and
    sorrows o'er,
And hand grasps hand, and eye-lids fill, and lips meet
    lips once more—
In that bright hour, perhaps—perhaps, some woman's
    voice would say—
"Think—think on those who weep to-night, poor exiles,
    far away!

www.ingramcontent.com/pod-product-compliance
Lightning Source LLC
Chambersburg PA
CBHW020759230426
43666CB00007B/764